MW00776992

WITHDRAWN

SWAN'S WAY

SWAN'S WAY

HENRI RACZYMOW *Translated from the French by* ROBERT BONONNO

NORTHWESTERN UNIVERSITY PRESS
EVANSTON, ILLINOIS

Northwestern University Press
Evanston, Illinois 60208-4210

Published 2002 by Northwestern University Press. English translation
copyright © 2002 by Robert Bononno. Originally published in French
under the title *Le Cygne de Proust*. Copyright © 1989 by Éditions Gallimard.
All rights reserved.

Printed in the United States of America

10 9 8 7 6 5 4 3 2 1

ISBN 0-8101-1925-0

Library of Congress Cataloging-in-Publication Data
Raczymow, Henri, 1948–
    [Cygne de Proust. English]
    Swan's way / Henri Raczymow ; translated from the French
by Robert Bononno.
        p. cm.
    ISBN 0-8101-1925-0 (alk. paper)
    1. Proust, Marcel, 1871–1922. Amour de Swann. 2. Haas, Charles
Nathan, 1832 or 3–1902. I. Title.
PQ2631.R63 A9837 2002
843'.914—dc21

                                                            2002011407

❋ *To Annette* ❋

Contents

SWAN'S WAY

First Impressions

A CAPE ("HOW I HAD LONGED TO WEAR ONE LIKE IT"), LACED boots and a monocle, a blue-and-pink oriental scarf, which he had bought because it was identical to the one on the Virgin of the Magnificat, a top hat lined with green leather. The Duchesse de Guermantes: "How clever to line one's hat in green."

An old clubman: "Tightly wrapped in a pearl gray redingote, which emphasized his height, svelte in his white gloves with black stripes, he wore a gray top hat that Delion made exclusively for him, the Prince de Sagan, Monsieur Charlus, the Marquis of Modena, Charles Haas, and Comte Louis de Turenne."

Someone other than myself might refer to this mingling of fiction and reality as a Balzacian process, intended to heighten the sense of truth. The artistry here lies in juxtaposing Swann and Haas in the same sentence to better signify that, although the first is not the second, they both belong to a world of shared values. Yes, Swann and Haas have many unusual traits in common, which they share, moreover, with a handful of other people. But it would be unwise to confuse them. Not only would we be factually mistaken, we would misconstrue those very aesthetic principles we were trying so hard to promote.

To whom exactly, Swann or Haas, did this "effect"—the green-lined top hat—belong? "I can see him now with his gray top hat lined in green" (Proust to Céleste).

(Charlus is the great Balzacian in the story. But his love of Balzac is inherited directly from Swann.)

Gestures

WE READ THAT THE NARRATOR WOULD HAVE LIKED TO HAVE
been as bald as Swann. To heighten the resemblance, he pulled
his nose and rubbed his eyes, the way a child does (one of Swann's
customary gestures, which he inherited from his father, was to
wipe his eyes and pass his hand over his forehead several times,
a sign of weariness). But how did Proust know that Swann—
Swann, not Haas—was bald, when Haas himself had never
been bald? This is not invention; he's contradicting himself.
There are several passages where Proust describes the short, red-
dish blond hair that is sometimes crimped (the crimps softened
the intensity of his green eyes, although elsewhere, speaking of
Gilberte's features, he remarks that she inherited her father's
"solid frankness of expression," in which liveliness never connoted harshness—another contradiction). Proust is insistent,
however. "His long, slightly bald head caused those who knew
of his success to remark, 'he's not handsome in any conventional
way, but he's chic with that tuft of hair, that monocle, and that
smile of his.'" Swann bald? Proust introduces a feature—an arbitrary one—that will distance him from Haas, obscure Haas.
But he chose the most unlikely of all.

HAAS HAD A CHARACTERISTIC GESTURE he made using the last three
fingers of his hand. Apparently this was a gesture of considerable

elegance. Let's see. The last three fingers. I hold out my hand and fold the index and thumb to form a circle. The remaining three fingers are extended, a bit like a fan. To what does this gesture (which isn't quite so elegant after all) correspond? When did Haas use it? I examine my hand. Then, suddenly, I recall someone from my childhood who made this same gesture. Someone who is still alive. I'll have to ask him if he remembers making this gesture, and under what circumstances he extended those three fingers. Of course, it would be ridiculous to question him about what was no more than a nervous tic, the way we might raise our eyebrows or scratch our ear, or smirk. Yet I suspect there's more to it than this. Although I can't prove it, something leads me to believe that the gesture is typically Jewish. Like a Yiddish phrase uttered in complicity, a password, an allusion designed purely for tribal use that remains unnoticed by outsiders. Did Haas's gesture, the gesture of the person from my childhood, serve a communicative function? Very likely. But I'm unaware of its significance. Or perhaps it meant nothing more than "Wait a moment. Don't say a word. Listen. . . . Let's assume that . . . I've got an idea."

This calls to mind someone else. His name is Jacques Sabbath. He's dead now, but I used to visit him in his office. That would have been ten years ago. He used this same gesture. There was also a neighbor on our floor, when I was a child and living on rue de la Mare. Daniel Zalsberg. Mountain of salt. I also recall seeing it used by a fellow student at school, whose name was Rozenberg. Mountain of roses. Rozenberg had freckles and was an excellent soccer player. He used to extend those three fingers of his hand whenever he wanted to argue with you or convince you of something. I see the gesture again, without being able to attach a face to my uncertain memory, used by a member of a small Trotskyist cell when I was twenty. I'm no longer certain whether he was Sephardic or Ashkenazy, but he was one or the other for sure. . . . I'm firmly convinced there's nothing elegant about this gesture. It's a Jewish gesture. Like the residual intonation of some buried jargon we retain.

It's the narrator's mother who notices this. Swann doesn't wipe his eyes—"just like his father"—as frequently as he once did. It must have been some other gesture. It doesn't matter. That person from my childhood, who also made a circle with his thumb and index finger, and whom I was reluctant and ashamed to identify, is my father.

Swann's gesture of wiping his eyes is a sign of fatigue, withdrawal. In *In Search of Lost Time*, Swann's fatigue is one of the leitmotifs used to announce his death. He grows tired of talking or listening, of being witty. He pulls out his handkerchief, wipes his glasses, and brushes his hand across his forehead and eyes. Go ahead without me. I'll be with you shortly. A momentary fatigue. It's nothing.

A Clubman

Swann's name had become almost mythological for me
. . . how I longed to hear it spoken.

THERE ARE SEVERAL SWANNS, JUST AS THERE ARE SEVERAL
characters in each of Proust's characters and several personae in
each of us. Several. Successively and simultaneously. There's the
Swann of Combray, indifferent or an object of hostility. There's
the fascinating figure of Gilberte's father. From the point of view
of the grandfather or the narrator's parents, there is "young
Swann" and the "Jockey Club Swann," about whom the father
once remarked, "Swann, with his ostentation, his insistence on
letting the whole world know about his most tenuous acquaintances, was a vulgar windbag whom the Marquis de Norpois
would have found, as he put it, 'putrid.'" (In general we would
be wise to display caution regarding the opinions of the various
Marquis de Norpois—past, present, and to come.) There is another Swann, however, one "who carried modesty and discre-
tion to the extremes of refinement in his social relations" and
graciously concealed an invitation from Twickenham or Buck-
ingham Palace. This Swann was both a boor and the epitome of
refinement. These two characteristics evolved with time. Swann
changed imperceptibly from the first to the second, achieving
equilibrium at the midpoint of his life, when both traits, boorishness and refinement, had equal weight. Proust is very explicit
about this: the evolution of his character is linked to the evolv-
ing status of his Jewishness. The more Jewish he becomes, the

more snobbish and vulgar, similar to Bloch. The less of a Jew he is, the more refined he becomes. He need only be simple. Except for one thing. His "simplicity" is but a more refined form of vanity. The narrator assumes this: Swann conceals a letter from Twickenham he supposedly has in his pocket. Twickenham, where, as the publicist Henri Rochefort noted, the exiled Comte de Paris sometimes invited Charles Haas.

Haas went through considerable trouble to gain admission to the Jockey Club. Proust knew all about this. "Ah, Céleste, Charles Haas! . . . He was the son of a stockbroker and, along with the Rothschilds, the only Jew to be admitted to the Jockey Club for his heroic conduct during the War of 1870."

It was after 1865 that Haas submitted his request for admission to the Jockey Club. He failed four times and was finally admitted on his fifth attempt. Of all the men who applied, he holds the record for perseverance. Which is why, during this period of his life in any case, snobbery took precedence over pride. He was finally accepted on January 21, 1871, apparently because of his valor during the war. Just like Charles Swann. And with good reason: many things were claimed of Charles Haas simply because Proust had said them about Charles Swann. It's a fascinating process, which, unlike the opposite and more conventional approach to art, uses fiction to inform reality.

Concerning Haas's accomplishments during this war, we know nothing. In fact, something tells me that there was nothing unquestionably heroic about them and that they probably amounted to nothing at all. I have little to go by, it's true, merely the fact that the idea of military heroism doesn't seem to stick well to this character. In 1871 Paris must have been in a state of considerable disorder. Sedan had collapsed, Paris was without food, the middle class had fled. I believe that Haas took advantage of this situation, after his many failures, to get himself admitted surreptitiously to the club amid the subdued turmoil of a deserted Paris. It's true that the club continued to function during the siege. Naturally, one didn't eat as well as before. But for forty francs members of the circle could buy an entire rabbit, which led his friend Galliffet to refer to the Jockey Club as "the society for the encouragement of the multiplication of rabbits."

On May 25, 1871, when the army's advance troops had penetrated Paris, General Galliffet was served dinner in the company of the members of the Jockey Club, some of whom belonged to his staff. On the menu was a fricassee made of rabbits that had been raised by the club during the siege.

ON RUE SCRIBE HAAS WAS SPONSORED by the Comte de Saint-Priest and Comte Albéric de Bernis. During his induction he is supposed to have said, "I am the only Jew to be accepted by Parisian society without being immensely rich" (that is, unlike the Rothschilds). I am strongly inclined to believe that Haas's comment is apocryphal, even though accurate. For these are the very same, or nearly the same, words used by Proust. Moreover, the word "Jew" seems unlikely here, out of place. Even more so since it was a Jew who said it. The more common term was "Israelite," which was not quite as harsh.

Comte Albéric de Bernis was a representative to the Chamber of Deputies from the Gard. In February 1898, shortly before the Zola trial, upon seeing Jaurès in the Chamber, he yelled, "You're the lawyer for the *syndicate!*" Pandemonium ensued. Invectives were hurled. Blows were exchanged. The count struck Jaurès. . . . It's true, this took place twenty-seven years later. But what do I care if Bernis became an anti-Dreyfusard, an anti-Semite in fact. What disturbs me more is Haas and his self-degradation, if only this once.

In Proust Swann's sponsors at the Jockey Club were General de Froberville and the Marquis de Bréauté. They were also said to have been his seconds at several duels. According to Proust scholars, these men are stand-ins for General Galliffet and the Marquis de Breteuil, both of whom were great friends of Haas. Together with Froberville, Swann frequented the Élysée Palace, and both men were "habitués of the Princesse des Laumes."

Catching sight of one another, they exchanged "a look of ironic and mysterious complicity," for both knew that they had compromised themselves through their association with the liberal Jules Grévy, the president of France during the Third Republic.

This business about the "syndicate" was a joke, a sign of Swann's humor. A *Witz*. Proust doesn't use the word *"Witz,"* though; he says "Jewish lightheartedness," adding that it was less subtle in Swann "than his urbane wit." To Proust, by definition, everything that is Jewish is debased. At the home of the Prince de Guermantes, Swann approaches Saint-Loup and the narrator, both Dreyfusards, "'Good evening,' he said to us. 'My God! All three at the same time. Someone's going to think it's a meeting of the syndicate. Pretty soon they're going to start looking for the cash register.'" This is not very "subtle." It's the kind of self-reflexive anti-Semitic humor typical of the Belle Époque, when Jews "lightheartedly" internalized everything that was said about them. Remember when Lévy met Kohn (or when Worms met Mayer or Wolf or Beer or Hirsch or Bloch or Weil or Cerf or Weiss or Schwartz or Berg or Blum or Dreyfus or Spire or Stern)? There followed a farcical, sidesplitting story of theft, money, and pretense. Where's the cash register?

Before the Jockey Club, Haas was a member of the Cercle de la rue Royale. In 1868 he appeared in Tissot's eponymous painting, along with Prince Edmond de Polignac, who would later marry a Miss Winaretta Singer, daughter of the sewing machine manufacturer. When my grandparents were alive, they used Singer sewing machines, which puts me on fairly good terms with the Prince de Polignac.

We know that Robert de Saint-Loup aspired to the Jockey Club. Within the context of his family background and social instinct, his desire is perfectly understandable. He did have one handicap, however. He was a Dreyfusard. And he was anxious for any information about his chances for admission. For example, he would have liked to know if Bloch belonged to the Cercle de la rue Royale. If some vulgar Bloch (a wonderful pleonasm if ever there was one) could be admitted to the Cercle, then there's no reason why the Jockey Club shouldn't admit me, Saint-Loup. The information turned out to be correct. The Guermantes considered the Cercle de la rue Royale "beneath their station" since it accepted Jews as members. And here was the proof. But for Haas this was not enough; he was worth more than any run-of-the-mill Jewish parvenu. The assumption was wrong, however. Bloch belonged only to the so-called Cercle des Ganaches, which was considered very far beneath their station indeed. But then, he was only Bloch.

Saint-Loup wrote to Swann to intercede with his old friend, the Duc de Mouchy, so he would vote for him at the Jockey Club. But the plan backfired. After the Dreyfus affair, Swann no longer set foot in the club. Haas, however, remained a member until his death in July 1902.

Rue Rabelais

THE JOCKEY CLUB USED TO HAVE A LIBRARIAN, A CERTAIN MLLE M———. Knowing this makes the institution a bit less intimidating to me. On the telephone she promises to look for titles that might be of interest. I find merely going to the building on rue Rabelais, opposite the Israeli embassy, to be quite disturbing. I am reminded of the uneasiness I felt when, as a young writer, I walked into the offices of the *Nouvelle Revue Française* for the first time. A feeling of radical alienation accompanied by a certain sense of advancement. But although I understand why I was, and continue to be, disturbed by the mere sight of the publishing company on rue Sébastien-Bottin, I have considerably more difficulty in understanding the attraction the club on the rue Rabelais, however prestigious (but for whom?), might have on me.

When I arrived, Mlle M———, an elderly teacher, blonde and friendly, vaguely reminded me of a Norman wet nurse who had looked after my daughter. I sat down at the end of a large table in an enormous room decorated with paintings of thoroughbred horses. She brought me five books and a sheet of note paper, embossed with the seal of the Jockey Club. Shortly after, a pleasant-looking young man sat down at the other end of the table. He immediately asked me if I were a "Proust fan." I've always had an aversion to what grammarians refer to as yes-no questions, those to which our only response can be yes or no, like certain social games. I hesitated before answering. I thought I could get out of it by blurting out, "Well, it's not exactly hero worship." The young man had already completed a study on comparative idleness among the bourgeoisie and the aristocracy in Proust. Magnificent! I spoke to him about Haas, with whom he was very familiar. Now we were on common ground. Everything there was to say about Haas's idleness got said. Just the day before, I had found, in the *Memoirs* of Boni de Castellane, a passage with the astonishingly modern title "How I Discovered America" (1924), a portrait—half in jest, half in earnest—of Charles, which could just as easily have applied to either Haas or Swann, and which, if not so mean spirited, could have come from Proust (or one of his characters). I had transcribed the passage in my notebook and, sensing it would be provocative, read it to the young man:

At the Comédie-Française we also met Charles Haas, a marvel of intuition, subtlety, and intelligence. Shy because of his Jewishness, he was the only one of his race who was poor, on good terms with women, fussed over in the salons, and sought out by men of worth. His was the kind of lazy and unproductive mind that was considered a luxury in the society of the time and whose principal merit consisted in predinner gossip at the "Jockey" or at the Duchesse de la Trémoille's salon. Although his failure to hold a job was not a matter of principle, his intelligence would have been sufficient justification for his ambition.

And what about the young man? Why was he so interested in all this? He was working on a doctorate on the origin of horse-racing associations. He intended to apply to his field of research the modern principles of historical methodology. In that case, I thought, better not contradict him. Once he corrected me, "No. It wasn't the Baron de M—— but the count." Or the opposite, I'm no longer certain. But I was caught and accepted my fate. In the end, he recommended two books, one

of which was entitled something like *Snobbery and Belles Lettres*. . . .
I've forgotten the title of the second. He also gave me a very
good definition, which I quickly copied into my notebook. "A
Jockey Club is any association whose members are not always
unhappy that others do not belong to it." This maxim reminded
me of a *Witz* by none other than Groucho Marx, who had been
invited to become a member of a "very exclusive" club. Groucho
answered with feigned alarm, "I don't want to belong to any
club that would have me as a member."

Swann's Name

THE LARGE QUESTION OF DETERMINING IF SWANN IS HAAS, IF the beautiful swan is in reality nothing but a common hare, won't be addressed here. At least not in such direct terms. Since I've already discharged myself of the question (a fine example of paraleipsis), thus relieving myself of its burden, I see no reason to provide a response.

In German, Haas is a hare. For a considerable length of time I thought, it seemed rather clear in fact, that I was chasing after a hare. Or rather a female: *hase* being a female hare in French. From this, beginning with the name Haas, resulted the ambiguous distribution of the sexes in the Proustian constellation. Have no fear, Haas was a ladies' man. Beyond a doubt. Proust says the same about Swann: "he was so fond of women, et cetera." And they were fond of him . . . more than fond. Degas, who was certainly jealous, complained bitterly about Haas's success with women. In fact, according to a well-founded rumor, it was the sight of certain women who were "former lovers of Haas" that so sickened Degas while he was taking the waters at Cauterets in the Pyrénées.

Given the inherent danger of flushing the hare too quickly, I thought this was a matter of some delicacy. A kind of incantation.

LIKE THE ROTHSCHILDS, Haas's father was born in the *Judengasse* of Frankfurt am Main. When Jakob Rothschild arrived in Paris, he changed his name to James. Not Jacques. Although I was unaware of the name of Haas's father at the time, I discovered that, once in Paris, he became Antoine. I later learned that he called his son Nathan, after his own father, who was Nathan Salomon. Similarly, Jakob Rothschild would become James de Rothschild and Proust would turn the too Germanic Haas into the very British Swann. Through some brilliant stroke of intuition, director Volker Schlöndorff chose an English actor, Jeremy Irons, to play Swann. He did this not so much because of Swann but because of Haas. "Jeremy Irons," the director is quoted as saying, "has that sense of British elegance, wit, and finesse generally attributed to Charles Haas."

The Café Anglais, located on the *Grands Boulevards* of Paris, was one of the multitude of symbols of the nineteenth century's Anglomania. Proust's Anglomania was concentrated in the character of Odette. In Nice, where she had once lived, it is said that her mother had given her, while practically a child, to a rich Englishman. As for Swann, his close relationship with the Prince of Wales was a secret in name only. He didn't boast of it. It was sufficient that people knew. Haas dined with the Prince of Wales at Paillard in Paris, along with the Marquis du Lau. There were women as well.

Proust, rather conveniently, anglicized Haas to make him less German—that is, less Jewish—and, paradoxically, more French. It was important that this Frenchification not be too overt. That would have been clumsy. So, the son of Nathan Salomon Haas rather suddenly became Antoine Haas. While this did nothing to eliminate his accent à la Nucingen, being English did allow for equivocation. It shifted Haas's foreignness from something that was pejorative (Jewish *and* "Boche") to something that was not merely acceptable but *fashionable*, something with prestige and snob appeal: England. For Jakob Rothschild to have become Baron James was a stroke of brilliance. Proust, intuitively no doubt, displays even greater genius when he creates Swann out of Haas (sociology) and turns a hare into a swan (aesthetics).

It's true, Haas and Swann speak without an accent—after all, they were born in France. But "Mother Moser," Swann's mother (or grandmother; it's never really clear), used to say, "Ponchour Mezieurs," a sound that had more to do with some German *Judengasse* than Oxford Street. Then there's the problem of Norpois. Through some perfidious unconscious tic, he insists on calling Odette "Madame *Svann*" (rather than Souann), thus consigning the name, against all expectation, to a ghetto from which it did not originate, but from which the man who bore it, albeit a fictional character, had only barely escaped. By insisting on calling her Madame *Svann*, Norpois renders null and void the procedure by which Haas, father and son, won their emancipation from a past as obscure Jews from Frankfurt into full-fledged French citizens. He also nullifies that same arc, that same broken line, refracted and parallel to reality, through which Proust accompanies and reinscribes as fiction, the passage from a German Jewish Hare to an Israelite in the process of being rapidly assimilated as a Swan by means of this clever and elegant detour through the English language.

And then there is Gilberte. You may recall that, after the death of her father, she succeeded in getting herself adopted by Monsieur de Forcheville, officially becoming Mademoiselle de Forcheville, and signing her letters G. S. Forcheville, a signature in which she gave, says Proust, "a particular importance to the S by turning it into a kind of long tail crossing the G." I will refrain from trying to interpret that long serpentine tail found in the first letter of Swann's name as it crosses the narrow mouth of his daughter's G. But she commits a curious faux pas with respect to her father's name, one of which the narrator is aware. A double-barreled, brightly blushing blunder. The narrator happens to discover that a young girl had asked Gilberte the name of her real father (since everyone knew that Forcheville was the name of her adoptive father). "In her confusion, and to minimize what she was about to say, she pronounced it Svann, rather than Souann, a change that she soon after discovered to be pejorative, since the pronunciation changed the name from English to German." It's all there in Proust, you simply have to read him.

But let's continue. Gilberte grows flustered, and because of her confusion, she betrays herself. And by betraying her father, she ghettoizes him and acknowledges her own (unmentionable) origins. What a remarkably resilient family. Yet, not a word is spoken. The word—cuts. Like an abscess it was the inevitable sign of some disorder: the tabooed German name. But why was a German name considered pejorative? We know that the Guermantes had considerable German blood in them. But in the case of Swann, it was clear that German meant Jewish. As in Balzac.

There is no mystery, however, about the fact that Gilberte was ashamed of her father, of her father's name. Yet, there's something mysterious about her past. Proust limits himself to the facts. "She frequently dissimulated her origins. Perhaps it was simply too unpleasant for her to admit them and she preferred that they learned about them from someone else. . . . By calling herself Mademoiselle de Forcheville, did she think they would forget she was Swann's daughter?" Proust, faithful in his own way, allows an enigmatic aura to cling to his characters and limits himself to the facts: Gilberte was ashamed of her dead father, of their name, but he seems incapable of providing the reason, thus revealing everything that is absurd in this aversion—an aversion altogether subsequent to the existence of the object of shame— since, and quite aside from the fact that any young woman her age could, if she had wanted to, have found out simply by asking someone older than herself, absolutely no one was unaware of the fact that Mademoiselle de Forcheville was Mademoiselle Swann. I mentioned Proust's manner, often discussed, of advancing a behavior, a type of speech, an ideology, and so forth, and attaching thirty-six thousand explanations to it, one as plausible as the next, without promoting one of them as most probable. Yet, in the matter of this belated, retrospective shame that Swann inspires in his daughter, Proust is silent. We must flounder by ourselves, left to our own lucubrations . . . or indifference.

How then can we explain Gilberte's inexplicable blushing? The mystery is always the same. Proust says that she blushed when certain names, such as that of her father, were uttered in her presence, including the amply connoted name of Lady Rufus Israels. Within this confection, the word "Lady," both noble and English, has difficulty softening "Israels," indecent, foreign, disturbing, as obvious as Swann's Jewish nose (and with reason, since she was his aunt), planted in the center of an otherwise perfectly agreeable face. Parisian high society saw in Swann, "an elegance that reigned in his face but stopped at his hooked nose, as if it had reached a natural border." Clearly, whether preceded by a title or not, it is unlikely that Lady Rufus's patronymic was very easy to bear, at least in certain circumstances or milieus. Still, why did Gilberte blush at the sound of a far more neutral name; a name so neutral, inoffensive, *genteel*, and so frankly goy, that it is Gilberte herself who inadvertently blurts it out? Take, for example, the name of her father's friend (and that of Haas's longtime friend), the Marquis du Lau. The full name of this gentleman from Périgord, companion of Edward, Prince of Wales, and Charles Haas, was du Lau d'Allemans. (According to the Duc de Guermantes, Saint-Simon makes a comparison between a d'Allemans and a provincial cock.) This helps explain Gilberte's enigmatic reddening with respect to her origins: Israels and d'Allemans, Jewish and German. We could play with these names in the clever (sadistic) way children often do. Gilberte: a German Jew, a Jewish German, and so on. In truth, Gilberte is very well informed about her origins, which can be traced to the *Judengasse* of a German city. Yet not a word is spoken! Beneath the swan lies a hare. The verbal slip ("Svann") and Gilberte's red cheeks are palimpsests.

Sadism, Death

> Swann's punchinello nose, which had long been
> absorbed by a pleasant face, now appeared enormous,
> swollen and crimson, more like that of an old Jew.

A HARSH, POSTHUMOUS SELF-PORTRAIT: "A PROPHET'S BEARD
dominated by an immense nose that dilates to draw in a final
breath."

In Proust's description of the ailing Swann, there is an obvious sense of complacency in disfiguring his character, in emphasizing his physical degradation. A form of revenge. For Proust's
description of Swann's "Jewishness" can hardly be called com-
plimentary. Swann regresses to an earlier and lower stage of his
evolution/ascension—that of his parents. A total collapse for
which the puppeteer shows no compassion. Nothing more than
a kind of sly pleasure. But why? It appears that at this moment
Proust was motivated by hatred. Self-hatred? Of course. *Selbst-
hasse.* We're not far from our hare here. Hatred of the Jew inside?
Let's not jump to conclusions. No. Revenge. From a strictly social point of view, Haas was more successful than Proust. But
Swann became a "Jew" again, he returned to square one—
nonexistence. Proust, however, cannot become a Jew again; he
never was one. But he has the ability to define a private identity,
an identity of identities, where identity itself is uncertain and
changeable, and sometimes moving—the identity of the writer.
This would be, this will be, his victory, leaving Swann/Haas far
behind him. Yes, it's possible that Proust might (only) have been

Swann/Haas. Which explains his anger about the fact that he was almost nothing more than this, that he had failed completely. Proust, the socialite, the pure "empty frame for a masterpiece," the man who could have chosen not to create, but to remain the spoiled, snobbish, and elegant son of a Jewish mother with a German name, was relentless in his attack on Swann and on himself.

He was literally relentless toward the ailing Swann. He savored his death. We might even say that Proust put him, Swann, to death. A corrida, a sacrifice, in the ritualistic and religious sense. Proust sacrificed the element of Swann/Haas in himself: the life in society, the vain ambitions. The religion that required this sacrificial rite was obviously Art. As with other religions, Art has its own rituals for sacrificing an expiatory victim. Proust could have restricted himself to prayer, which, in the context of Judaism, replaced the "bestial" sacrifice that was still tinged with paganism. Or in the case of Christianity, both prayer and the theatrical metaphor of sacrifice embodied in the Eucharist and transubstantiation. But this was not the case. Neither Jew nor truly Christian, Proust chose to "regress" to a more primitive form, one that was still not entirely dissociated from archaic paganism—the slaughter of an animal. The slaughter of the beautiful swan of flesh and blood, consecrating the coming of the abstract Sign, from now on the only object of worship, was the very object Swann/Haas did not want to or was unable to approach. This was the apogee of modernity (following Flaubert and Baudelaire): God is dead (or at least, with the arrival of mechanization and progress, dying peacefully amid our general indifference). All that remained was religion, a mixture of paganism (in its rites) and the preservation of the principle of a revealed religion, of transcendence, which, in this case, was Art.

Concerning Proust's sadistic relentlessness with respect to Swann's physiology and his appearance after his illness, the following two passages in the novel are worth noting.

The first concerns the grocer—pleasant enough toward Gilberte and Marcel—who ran the stall on the Champs-Élysées: "It was from her that Swann always bought his *pain d'épice*, which for health reasons he ate a great deal of, since he suffered from chronic eczema and was as constipated as the Prophets." This idiosyncrasy is cause for reflection. Coming from Madame Verdurin, such a disclosure would have been understandable. Or from Charlus when he let himself go. (The following remark is occasionally cited as an example of Proust in a moment of indiscretion: "As for all those little fools with their fancy names—the Marquis de Cambremerde or the Marquis de Vatefairefiche—there is no difference between them and the greenest recruit in your regiment. Whether you visit the Comtesse Caca to take a leak or the Baronne Pipi to take a shit, it all amounts to the same thing." But we would be wrong in our assumption. For it is not Proust who is speaking here, but Charlus, addressing Morel. Moreover, Proust adds, it is Charlus making a fool of himself. Although Proust sits in the background applauding wildly, he manages to stigmatize Swann's snobbery when he boasts of being a friend of the Comte de Paris, whereas the princes, the true princes, were devoid of snobbery. They drifted above the pathetic vanity of people such as Swann, or Verdurin, or even Proust.) And yet . . . through his "Prophets' constipation," and in spite of the capital P, I have caught Proust in a compromising position with vulgarity. He has yielded to the pleasure of a word that is both effortless and gratuitous, and in doubtful taste, and he is too lazy to place the word in the mouth of a more fictively likely character, one who would have some reason to utter it. Proust reduces Swann to a little Jew who is both pretentious and insignificant—the only thing he has in common with the prophets is constipation. But we would have no way of knowing that they were afflicted with such a disorder. Here Proust tarnishes what he loves most and reveres. He is Mademoiselle Vinteuil spitting on her father's photograph.

Isn't there something suspicious about this vulgarity, this blasphemy, where Swann and the prophets of Israel are lumped together and ingested during a single and laborious act of defecation?

The second passage refers to an event that occurs toward the end of the novel, when, during a visit to the Prince and Princesse de Guermantes, Proust writes that Swann's face "was dotted with small spots of Prussian blue . . . and he gave off the kind of odor that, at school . . . makes it so unpleasant to remain in the 'science' laboratory."

The elegant Swann is dead from this moment on. Proust has begun to destroy him. In actuality, however, he began much earlier, with his tale of constipation and the prophets, where, in keeping with the Wagnerian manner of Proust's art, Swann's death is already prefigured. But perhaps this involves more than just art. For Swann, the dead Swann, will still share something with the prophets: a beard, "dominated by an immense nose." And his (new) affection for (other) Jews. It is at this moment that Proust puts him to death. And it was under similar circumstances that Haas gave up the ghost. But the true "prophet," the one for whom speech is a creative act, is unquestionably Proust, and Proust alone.

It is significant that Gilberte would later inflame the wound that Proust had introduced, intensifying his sadistic pursuit of Swann. She managed this through a character trait that I still do not entirely understand, since Swann was an influential figure and dearly loved his daughter—a feeling of shame about her father and of their common name, which made her blush every time she heard it. I cannot understand Gilberte. I would have been pleased if my daughter had a father like Charles Swann.

I find an echo of this death-dealing sadism when Charlus—this is hardly surprising coming from him—announces "with almost triumphant callousness . . . 'Hannibal de Bréauté, dead! Antoine de Mouchy, dead! Charles Swann, dead! Adalbert de Montmorency, dead! Boson de Talleyrand, dead! Sosthène de

Doudeauville, dead! . . .' And each time," adds Proust, "the word 'dead' seemed to fall upon the deceased like a heavy shovelful of earth, thrown by a grave digger intent on driving them deeper into the grave."

A publicist such as Arthur Meyer, in his column for *Le Gaulois*, would not have failed to place Charles Swann/Haas at the end of this list. Even Charlus, if he were to be consistent with social usage, would have had to mention Swann last. People will say that he lists the names in the order they come to mind. Obviously. But it is Proust writing. Proust is the only person who, in this list of the illustrious, and even notorious, deceased, has no reason to downgrade Swann. Yet, he places his name in the center of his list, as if the other names formed a halo around it. Death is the great leveler, and Swann has once and for all joined his peers from the Jockey Club.

Who is this grave digger, determined to triumph in the pursuit of his obligations? It is Proust the writer, who will not rest until he has buried the dead, only to save them by naming them in his book. To save their strange, archaic, and slightly barbarous names for a while longer.

S/Z

CHARLUS, OF COURSE, WAS FULLY AWARE OF ALL THIS. ESPECIALLY about the Jews. For at the time, Jews and homosexuals were both considered pariahs. One day Charlus grew curious about Bloch and asked the narrator for his address. The narrator recalled that his father's offices had been located on rue des Blancs-Manteaux. In reality there was no reason for Charlus to have been familiar with this neighborhood, which for him was both eccentric and inconvenient. And yet . . . he remarks that the area is not far from Paris's own *Judengasse.* [*Sic.*] Which would be rue des Rosiers. This is rather startling coming from Charlus, this use of a German word to designate a Jewish street and its geographic location. What he may not have known, however, was Bloch's literary pseudonym and the name he was about to officially adopt: Jacques du Rozier. A quasi-Freudian slip involving the *Judengasse* itself, with the inclusion, moreover, of that *z* that both Bloch and Proust could easily have done without. But the temptation was too great. From Rosiers to Rozier, Albert Bloch, the cousin of a cartoon Esther Lévy, made the transition from plural to singular, to singularity, from *s* to *z*, a *z* that was not so much untimely as superfluous, embodying an aggressive foreignness that draws attention to itself, like the endearing *"coucou"* innocently proclaimed by the cocotte in the street, which secretly and maliciously, compromises you. *S/Z?*

Roland Barthes wrote exquisitely about *S/Z*. His words are beautiful, although for me, somewhat obscure. For Barthes, *Z* was the letter of mutilation. It behaved "like a chastising whip . . . like an oblique and illegal blade. 'Z' cuts, crosses, slashes." With respect to the forward slash between *S* and *Z*, Barthes wrote that it was "a mark of censure, a specular surface."

By incorporating this *z* in du Rozier, Bloch mutilates and chastises himself. He effaces and censures his Judaism, castigates himself for being Jewish. It was his Jewish identity he no longer wanted to see reflected in that "specular surface." Yet I still fail to understand Barthes's use of the verb "cut." What could Bloch have cut that hadn't been already? And then, I recall again Gilberte's signature once she had become Mademoiselle de Forcheville: G. S. Forcheville, a signature in which, Proust wrote, the tail of the *S* in Swann had "crossed" the *G* in Gilberte. Of course, this *S* isn't exactly a *Z*, but it's close enough. And doesn't it belong to Barthes's paired *S/Z*? For it served the same purpose of "cutting, crossing, and slashing." And Proust specifically says "cross." It was indeed the *S* in Swann that caused Gilberte to blush inexplicably.

Swan: To the Letter

THE SIGNIFIER "SWAN" APPEARS TWICE IN *IN SEARCH OF LOST TIME*. Once in a literary-amorous context, the other in a mythological-erotic context.

The narrator writes a good-bye letter to Albertine in which he evokes, in the past conditional, the modalities of a shared life together: Albertine would have had her own car and a yacht. "The yacht is almost ready and will be called, as you requested in Balbec, *The Swan* . . . I'll have those verses of Mallarmé you liked so much engraved on the . . . of the yacht. . . . Do you remember? It's the poem that begins 'The virginal, vibrant, and beautiful today.'"

The "swan" is also the curve of Albertine's thigh looking for the mouth of some Leda.

In the *Search*, the swan is literature and desire, literature as desire and pleasure. The *Search* is the story of substitution, the narrator's substitution of bodily desire with literary desire.

As a name Swann serves as a metaphor for the love of "life." In Proust "life" is always surrounded by quotation marks. For at bottom, the narrator doesn't know much about "life" ("the beauty of life, a word somehow deprived of meaning, something not quite yet art, where I had seen Swann pause"), at least about what others refer to as "life." What do they mean? To live. Life is, well, life. Everyone knows what it is. The little milkmaid whom the narrator asks to run an errand for him: "I felt that she was about to say that she, 'liked sports' and that in a few years she would say that she was, 'living her own life.'" "Life" is merely a tautology.

Swann is the character who finds "life" curious. How strange. He contaminates Charlus. "I don't work for history, life is sufficient for me, it is sufficiently interesting, as poor Swann used to say." But in loving "life," Swann ruins it. Ruins himself. Swann is a failure. His consolation, his alibi and excuse, Proust says, is to pretend to believe that "life" is a novel.

Tissot, Painter

IT WAS A BEAUTIFUL SPRING DAY AND I HAD JUST TURNED FORTY. I began my inquiry by going to the Bibliothèque de l'Arsenal, arriving at three minutes before ten, which is when it opens. There is a small square in front of the building with a sculpture of Arthur Rimbaud, "the man who sings on his feet." The idea flashed through my mind that the sculptor who had engraved those words had made a foolish error. And in fact someone had corrected the inscription, replacing "who sings on his feet" by "with wings on his feet." That evening I read an article in *Le Monde* about the inauguration by Minister Jack Lang of the statue of Captain Dreyfus in the Tuileries Gardens: "The veil has fallen and Captain Dreyfus, an immense lead soldier, gripping the handle of his broken sword, appears. The honor of the officer who was so wrongly condemned has been washed in the bronze of statues."

Turning the page, I read that "in front of the Arsenal stood an afflicted Rimbaud, 'the man who sings on his feet,' the result of a bad pun." This explained it. What I had thought to be a mistake (and the anonymous corrector along with me) was simply a play on words. My stupidity annoyed me, and the bad pun didn't make it any better.

I had come to look at an issue of *L'Illustration* in which appeared a reproduction of a painting by James Tissot, *The Balcony of the Cercle de la Rue Royale* (1868). In June 1922 Paul Brach had sent this same reproduction to Proust. The painting had been displayed as part of an exhibition on the Second Empire and portrayed the Prince de Polignac, the Marquis du Lau, Galliffet, and Charles Haas. Obviously I felt estranged from that superlatively worldly group, the *Almanach de Gotha's* upper crust, which appeared in the poor reproduction. What was I doing, examining this Areopagus? My feelings ranged from alienation to disgust and were channeled through my anguish in the face of the disturbing evidence before me: when finally confronted by my subject, I instinctively felt little empathy for him. Suddenly, I noticed where Charles Haas was standing on the balcony. He was near the door, facing the others, a bit to the side, as if he were hesitant about joining them, penetrating deeper into their intimacy, entering the circle. Quite happy now, I said to myself, That's it! Haas was part of the Circle, but remained on the periphery. Something prevented him from crossing that invisible gap. I was able to identify the source of this exclusion: Haas was Jewish, did not have a title or a prestigious lineage, and no great wealth. He seemed to accumulate negative traits. It was at this moment that Haas became for me less distant, less foreign.

My aversion for Tissot was equally instinctive. Was he related to the famous Doctor Tissot, the immortal author of *Onanism, A Dissertation on the Diseases Caused by Masturbation* (1760)? But this Doctor Tissot was Swiss. And my painter was from Nantes. I discovered that he had been involved in the events of the Commune, which had forced him to go into exile in London, where he had become the official portrait painter of Victorian high society. He had changed neither his profession nor his style, and returned from England only in 1881. Later I learned something about Tissot that made him appear somewhat more sympathetic, at least temporarily. He had fallen victim to a mystical crisis and had taken off for Palestine. For several years he worked on illustrating the Bible, "painting only religious scenes," a caption read, "that contained great pseudo-archaeological detail." This "pseudo-archaeological detail" could also be applied to the paintings of high society he made during his life outside the fold.

Baudelaire says that, in the Church of Notre-Dame in Anvers, he saw a painting by James Tissot. However, "We do not know," wrote the author of the critical edition of Baudelaire I consulted, "whether Baudelaire actually saw any Tissot paintings in Anvers." He adds, "The remark is nonetheless quite interesting, for the painter had much in common with our poet." Now that was a worthwhile piece of information. Somewhat cryptic, I'll admit, for he never mentions exactly what they had in common.

Someone sent me a photocopy of the catalog of the painter's work. I read about the background of Tissot's canvas. One day twelve members of the Cercle de la rue Royale decided to have their portrait painted. They contacted Tissot, a successful painter, and each contributed a thousand francs to cover expenses. In deciding who would keep the painting, they drew lots; it went to Baron Hottinguer (1825–1920), the grandfather of the current owner. The Cercle gathered at 1 rue Royale, in one of the two buildings by the architect Gabriel at Place de la Concorde in Paris. The balcony, I read, did not belong to the Hotel Crillon but was part of the offices of President de Morgan and Company. From left to right, here are the names of the twelve individuals who posed for mortality:

Comte A. de la Tour-Marbourg
Marquis du Lau
Comte Étienne de Ganay
Comte J. de Rochechouart
C. Vansittard
Marquis de Miramon
Baron Hottinguer
Marquis de Ganay
Gaston de Saint-Maurice

Prince de Polignac
Marquis de Galliffet
Charles Haas

The catalog adds, "The last man seen in the doorway was one of the outstanding dandies of the time and has remained famous as the model for Proust's character, Swann."

Would I be able to locate Baron Hottinguer's grandson? I found him in the phone book. His first name was Rodolphe and he would have been over eighty. The voice of reason whispered to me that I wasn't going to call him.

"Madame Proust"

But I did call Bernadette A——, whose telephone number someone had given me and who hated being called "Madame Proust," which I of course had no intention of doing, limiting myself only—and this was already overdoing it—to remarking that she was a "Proustian," an eminent scholar. Our conversation couldn't have been more agreeable and was typical of those delightful exchanges between people when they discuss what they know best, and who are able to capture the slightest allusion, a name or telling detail, and reveal its source, the truth of a genealogy, or perhaps contradict some bit of information, completing the sentence the other has barely begun, in the very terms he or she would have used. There was a complicity between us, a kind of caress. This was unusual for me, especially with respect to Proust, and I imagined that for her, Bernadette A——, this must have been, on the contrary, something quite ordinary, since she was involved, on a daily basis, with others far more knowledgeable than I about Proust. During our discussions, I rediscovered the feeling of making love that came over me as an adolescent in the simple encounter with a girl with whom an exchange, even though purely intellectual, and indeed sentimental, was still possible. How foolish I was! So, we talked. Jacques Bizet, Madame Straus, Céleste Albaret, Albert Le Cuziat, Maurice Sachs, James Tissot. We extolled the merits of

Julian Barnes's book *Flaubert's Parrot*. My enjoyment in reading the book had led me to Haas, even though there was no direct connection between them. We discussed Tissot's painting. Bernadette was not unaware that it belonged to Baron Hottinguer. But I was unaware that his name was pronounced something like *Otingre*. I nearly fainted. She thought the painting was located in the Château de Guermantes, in Seine-et-Marne, which was owned by the Hottinguer family. She mentioned the "well-known" episode of drawing lots and grew enthusiastic about Haas's beauty, which provided an opportunity for me to discuss the torrid letters from Sarah Bernhardt (this, at least, I could be certain she was unaware of), the captivating Sarah, about whom Charles couldn't have cared less. Women threw themselves at his feet, from demimondaines to the female upper crust of the Tuileries and Compiègne: Mesdames de Pourtalès and de Metternich, Madame de Mouchy, the Princesse d'Essling. Moreover, in the Nadar photograph, Sarah, at the time of her relationship with Haas, was not very beautiful, although . . . no, she simply wasn't. And since I was speaking, I took advantage of the situation to ask about the Marcel Proust Prize. Did it include a residency at the Grand Hotel of Balbec, or rather Cabourg? No, there was a more prosaic award of a hundred thousand francs.

Taking her into my confidence, I expounded a bit on my true feelings, although I was aware of my clumsiness. A book about Haas, I remarked to Bernadette A——, might turn out to be impossible. I soon felt as if I had encountered a wall of unknowable. . . . Silence. Bernadette A—— was thinking. She would try to get as much information as possible from the universities and scholars. She would let me know.

She let me know: Haas would be of no interest to either the academic or the scholarly community. The subject was too anecdotal. And she herself was not far from that opinion. Did she think she had offended me? If so, she failed since I took her remark as a compliment. I would have exchanged everything I knew about Haas for it: the subject's *anecdotal* character was of no interest to scholars. Far from discouraging me, she confirmed the fact that the hare I was pursuing, and the hunt itself, were worth the effort.

I spent a few days, or maybe only a few hours, I'm no longer sure, dreaming about the Marcel Proust Prize, which "had become almost mythological for me." I imagined my residence at the Grand Hotel of Balbec as the pampered guest of the Princesse de Guermantes, de Parme, d'Agrigente (who were no less unlikely than Badoura, the famed princess of the *Thousand and One Nights*).

Swan Song

SWANN IS NOT HAAS.

When the first volume of *In Search of Lost Time* appeared, someone, Gabriel Astruc, recognized Haas. Proust, pretending to be surprised, asked, "What makes you think it was Haas?" He maintained his position, claiming this was impossible. In the first place, I don't do portraits. What's the use of wearing ourselves out writing, then, if all we do is copy reality? Yes, it's true Haas was the starting point for Swann. But "I filled him with an entirely different personality." It's also true that I could tell you a thousand and one stories about Haas. "I would be delighted to let you hear them." None of them appear in my book, however. And for good reason: there's nothing anecdotal in my book. Q.E.D.

A number of people recognized Haas. Madame Straus, for example. She had insisted on referring to Swann as Swann-Haas. How ridiculous! But Proust was upset. Swann is not Haas. There are no clues, no portraits, in my book.

When he related (related and not described) Swann's death, Proust used a false quotation from a real newspaper. He didn't specify which one, although he alluded to *Le Gaulois*, where "it was reported that Swann's health had caused concern." A phony obituary transcribed from an apparently real newspaper concerning a fictional character, Charles Swann. *There are no clues, no portraits, in my book.*

We have just learned the unfortunate news that M. Charles Swann passed away yesterday in his home in Paris following a painful illness. A Parisian whose wit was as widely appreciated as his discriminating yet steadfast friendship, he will be universally missed by everyone in the artistic and literary communities, where his refined taste ensured his popularity, as well as at the Jockey Club, where he was one of the oldest and most respected members. M. Swann also belonged to the Cercle de l'Union and the Cercle Agricole, and only recently resigned as a member of the Cercle de la rue Royale. His intelligent features and celebrity never failed to arouse public curiosity during any *great event* involving music or painting, or any of the "openings" at which he was a constant presence until recent years, when he rarely left his home. The funeral ceremonies will take place, et cetera.

Death has overtaken one of the best liked and most brilliant Parisians. M. Charles Haas, for years a welcome figure in the salons and clubs, passed away yesterday after a long and painful illness. He will be greatly missed, as both a gentleman and a brilliant conversationalist, by the Parisian society of which he was an integral part until recent years. His irreproachable elegance, his uncommon features, imbued with delicacy and mischief, his distinguished appearance, everything about him, in short, that made him a society favorite and reminded us of the heroes and heroines of a less barbarous age—the portrait of a Valois who has stepped down from his frame—contributed less toward his social success than his personal wit. M. Haas possessed an inexhaustible store of wit, a subtle and quintessentially French wit. He was an incomparable raconteur, a man with an amazing facility for storytelling, et cetera.

How can we tell the spurious from the authentic, the obituary written by Proust in *The Captive* from the one written by a certain Dancourt, which appeared in *Le Figaro* on Tuesday, July 15, 1902? Or whether the first concerns Charles Haas and the second Charles Swann?

In spite of the similarity of the two articles, even to the occasional use of identical expressions (passed away yesterday/passed away yesterday, a painful illness/a long and painful illness, until recent years/until recent years, his intelligent features/his uncommon features, et cetera), I am especially taken with Dancourt's parenthetical allusion to Haas as "the portrait of a Valois who has stepped down from his frame." This physical assimilation of Haas to a Valois also appears in Proust's description of Swann's face wasted by illness, during the evening at the Prince and Princesse de Guermantes's. His punchinello nose, he writes, "now looks . . . more like that of an old Israelite than of some eccentric Valois."

There is a very good possibility that Proust may have read this article about the death of Charles Haas in the *Figaro* of July 1902. But does it really matter? It was never my intention to show that Proust was wrong, or even that he may have lied, in writing "There isn't a single element of this book that is not a fiction, there isn't a single 'disguised' character. I invented everything as I saw fit." The simplest answer is that it was inconvenient for Proust to *avow* that Swann was Haas. This would have subtracted something from his divine assertion of creation ex nihilo. And yet, even as he denied this connection, he told Gabriel Astruc in December 1913 that "Haas is in fact the only person—not that I wanted to describe him per se—who was the starting point for my Swann (although I gave him an altogether different personality)." Was this a way for Proust to claim the contrary by confronting someone who knew Haas and could not have failed to make the identification with Swann?

When Swann's death was announced in "the newspapers," there followed in *The Captive* a reflection on death and its selective treatment according to title and status. Death does not equalize individual destiny. Far from it, said Proust. It continues, confirms, and reflects the inequality of the living. If you are, or were, the Duc d'Uzès, your staying power will be greater than if your name were that of a "fashionable bourgeois." And if Haas's—I mean Swann's—name has any likelihood of enduring, the credit belongs to me, Marcel Proust, author of a book in which it is clear that "the character of Swann possesses some of your traits." This is a strange and amusing way to put it. The fictional character Charles Swann, Proust *dixit*, possesses certain traits of Charles Swann! I've saved Swann—at least for a while, a long while though—from the oblivion to which death would have consigned him, because my book mentions you. Does that make Swann a real character? Or, rather, does that make this character a real person? Could Proust have been so careless as to have written "Some of Haas's traits appear in the character of Swann" without obviously contradicting himself? And put it in his book? He certainly could have written it in a letter. And he did mention it, not only to Gabriel Astruc, but to a Madame Hennessy, in 1917, and quite spontaneously, without the least provocation on her part, which is understandable since she had never known Haas and may not even have heard of him (by definition, there are always more people in this category). "Unlike poor Haas, whom you are too young to have known and whom I thought of from time to time when creating Swann, I am unable to claim that 'I am indifferent to quality but have a great fear of quantity.'" It would have been impossible to make that claim in the book. In the first place, "there isn't a single fact that isn't fictional," "there isn't a single disguised character," "I invented everything," and so on. But other factors, as important as internal consistency, come into play. For the book (like our Valois, who had become Haas) would then have stepped down from its frame and, like a river, have disappeared in the undifferentiated ocean of reality. A clumsy (and revealing) fusion and confusion would have occurred between art and that which is not art. And on that same page, Proust mentions Tissot's canvas "representing the balcony of the Cercle de la rue Royale, where you appear between Galliffet, Edmond de Polignac, and Saint-Maurice." Who, then, is this "you" Proust is addressing? Haas or Swann? Or some strange hybrid, some unknown monstrosity, which Madame Geneviève Halévy Straus, for whom such a creature seemed entirely plausible, insisted on calling Swann-Haas?

What's more, Proust is incorrect: you are not standing *between* Galliffet, Edmond, and the others. You may not be standing alone, but you are certainly on the periphery of the group, on the threshold. . . .

We can provide a fairly precise estimate of the moment when Proust "reinfused" (which is how he referred to his many additions to the text) this passage concerning Swann's death into the *Search*. It was written after the fact, sometime shortly before his own death. Tissot's canvas had been reproduced in the June 10, 1922, issue of *L'Illustration* in conjunction with an exhibition held at the Musée des Arts Décoratifs entitled "Decoration during the Second Empire." Proust's friend Paul Brach had sent him the reproduction. Proust knew that he hadn't much time left; he died five months later, on November 18, 1922. Swann's death, which he returned to a few months before, prefigured his own. Will his name endure? This man who is neither prince, nor marquis, nor the Duc d'Uzès? Yes, most definitely yes! Even though you are not the Duc d'Uzès, there's still a chance your name will live on. But on one condition only: that you have managed to "produce." Proust says, in reference to Swann, "Although he 'produced' nothing, he was lucky enough to survive a while longer." An absurd statement, then and now. For it would mean accepting Swann as a real person, rather than a character in a book, a creature without organs, as Valéry described the Venus de Milo.

But Proust did "produce"; he will survive. At least, for a while longer. And in this way, *The Captive*, the book in which Swann dies, is Proust's swan song. Proust may not be the Duc d'Uzès, but then neither is he merely a "very fashionable bourgeois."

The names of those very fashionable bourgeois break apart and dissolve as soon as they die. Swann was . . . a remarkable intellectual and artistic personality, and although he "produced" nothing, he was fortunate enough to live on a while longer. And yet, dear Charles Swann, although I never knew you very well when I was so young and you were so close to death, it's because the youngster you must have considered a little idiot made you the hero of one of his novels that people are beginning to talk about you again and that you may perhaps live on.

In the following sentence, however, incongruity and absurdity are cranked up another notch:

> The fact that people are talking so much about your presence in Tissot's canvas depicting the balcony of the Cercle de la rue Royale, where you are standing between Galliffet, Edmond de Polignac, and Saint-Maurice, results from the similarities between yourself and the character of Charles Swann.

Though I've exhausted myself trying to figure out the various meanings of this sentence, I've come to the conclusion that it simply doesn't make sense. I'm not gloating over the fact that Proust may have written something obscure, which I've managed to unearth. What caught my attention is the fact that it is precisely this sentence that doesn't ring true. There are two "mistakes" here: (1) the one already mentioned, "It's because of the similarities between yourself ('dear Swann') and the character of Charles Swann," and (2) I can't see the logical relationship between Tissot's canvas and the fact that people are talking about you so much. They certainly couldn't be talking about Haas, Haas or Swann—I'm completely lost here—*in* the painting. At best it would only be the Tissot reproduction, which appeared in 1922, that brought the name of Charles Swann/Haas to attention again. Proust's thinking here is a lot like Albertine's: his syntax breaks down whenever his reasoning gets sidetracked. What exactly does this tell us about his thought process? We will never really know. There is something, however, that this disturbance, this lie in the text, reveals. A few pages before this in *The Captive* Proust writes:

> But in her conversation . . . there appeared certain contradictions, certain adjustments, that were, to me, quite obvious. This conversation was characterized—not out of any

concern for style, but to hide her carelessness—by those sudden syntactical leaps that resemble what the grammarians call anacolutha, or something to that effect.

Anacolutha so inextricably bound up with the thought and language processes common to both Proust and Albertine that although Proust's sentence "in Tissot's canvas" is unintelligible, it is still grammatically correct. This very unintelligibility is, moreover, reinforced by its correctness, and it is this very fact that disturbs, irritates, and delights me: this sentence, which is for me *so blatantly obvious,* signifies that the swan is here making a sign, calling out from beyond the grave or, rather, somewhere between death and the art that would spare him a while longer, spelling out, trying to spell his name in the hope that Proust will save him, in extremis.

(The work of art is not a sphere but only an approximation of one, just as the earth is, with its cracks, its crevices, and its "faults." Bataille says that desire arises when we catch sight of some secret and infinitesimal disfigurement on the supposedly "perfect" body of a woman. The cracks, crevices, and faults in the work of art are what enable us to grasp it, appropriate it, want to appropriate it, penetrate it, realize that it is possible to do so and that the work of art will not resist, and will even ask to be penetrated.)

But it was Robert Dreyfus who became aware of these "mistakes" long before I did. In 1909 Dreyfus produced a one-volume collection of articles, *Petite histoire de la revue de fin d'année,* that he had published earlier in the literary supplement to *Le Figaro,* between February 22 and June 6, 1908. He sent the collection to Proust, who answered him on June 29, "Your piece, played by Haas at Mouchy, had me in tears." Dreyfus had written about a performance, *Les Cascades de Mouchy,* given by the Marquis de Massa at the Château de Mouchy on December 19, 1863, in which Charles Haas appeared (along with the Comte and Comtesse Edmond de Pourtalès, the Marquis and Marquise de Galliffet, the Duc de

Mouchy, et cetera). Dreyfus, writing in 1909, was unable to understand Proust's statement of how the retelling of something that had occurred fifty years earlier, before either Dreyfus or Proust had been born, had brought Proust "to tears." "I had caught a glimpse of Monsieur Haas once before," he wrote, "a man whose wit, whose 'chic,' and whose gray hat were so Second Empire. Later on, when reading *Swann*, I realized that Haas had 'posed,' without knowing it, for the character of Swann." So it wasn't until 1913, when Proust's book appeared, that Robert Dreyfus was able to gauge his friend's extraordinary interest in the stylish man with the gray hat. But to the point of shedding tears over the retelling of a fairly trivial event? This is what *I* have such a hard time understanding. Couldn't it be said that Proust was, in retrospect, disproportionately and mythically in love with Haas? (We know, based on Proust's *Notebooks*, that it was initially Swann, not the narrator, who was to be the axis around which the book would revolve; *Swann in Love*, the novel within the novel, remained a vestige of the book's initial formulation. It was only later that Proust would divide Swann in two: into the character of Marcel and the character of Charles Swann, who was outside him but linked to him by so many identical traits.) Yet Proust never went to Charles Haas's funeral, which was attended by all of Parisian society: mass at Saint-François-de-Sales, burial at Père-Lachaise (while Swann was resting in peace in the fictional cemetery of words and paper in Combray: *In Search of Lost Time*).

It was with a mixture of sadness and joy (for out of vanity I would have liked to take credit for this discovery and I was, at the same time, happy to see it confirmed, and not by just anyone) that I realized that Robert Dreyfus had pointed out the same fictional inconsistency—the confusion, in this passage of *The Captive*, between the character of Haas and the character of Swann—in his *Souvenirs sur Marcel Proust* (1926):

> I have to agree, it's a very strangely constructed sentence in
> its enigmatic negligence . . . all that is needed is to replace

the name of Charles Swann with that of Charles Haas. It goes without saying that Tissot could not have introduced Swann's fictional face into the balcony of the Cercle de la rue Royale. But at the Second Empire exhibition held in 1922 (six months before Proust's death), everyone saw the painting in which the artist immortalized the effigy of the elegant Monsieur Haas.

This all makes very good sense. One expression, however, doesn't quite ring true: "immortalize." A rather hasty judgment it would seem. For if people are again talking of Haas, of which Proust was justifiably proud, it's because of Swann. And if everyone was so surprised by James Tissot's canvas, which was exhibited in Paris in May 1922, it was also because of Swann. Proust, that is. Everyone ran to see the "model." Without Proust, without Swann, there would have been no reason ever to have mentioned Haas again, and Tissot's canvas would have been considered for what it is, a fashionable but insignificant painting. Without Proust, Haas would have remained anonymous after his demise. The lines in the newspaper announcing his death, lines that Proust pretended to transcribe (which he, in fact, almost transcribed), "managed to turn a *living* being . . . into nothing more than a *name*, a written *name*," a living being reduced to *a* name (the indefinite article speaks volumes here), a *written* name. A name that soon, after having circulated a while in conversation, would cease even to be pronounced. And no one doubted that Proust was thinking not of Swann but of Haas when he wrote, "A book is an enormous cemetery where the names have been worn away on the tombstones." We can no longer read Haas's name on Swann's "tombstone," for Swann's character is itself a tomb where, in a kind of cruel paradox, Haas's anonymity lies. Time, oblivion, the death of contemporaries turn the work of art into a palimpsest of reality. This is, perhaps, why the humble biographer, the conscientious ant working on his unwilling enterprise, the biographer that I am not, is a kind of scavenger or, rather, carrion beetle: not only does he deal in death, but he needs death to ensure that his subject is sealed and bound forever, like the side of meat to which it has now been reduced (and as if he required further proof, his steps lead him, before all else, to the tomb where it lies); but at the same time, he challenges this death, is horrified by it, and tries to circumvent it, as if, through his own work, he could deny it.

Proust's notion of the "book as cemetery" is quite unexpected. It is a sign and a proof of something he always tried to deny, both in his correspondence and in his writing: that his work was in some sense dependent upon reality. "On the contrary," he continued, "we remember the name quite clearly but without knowing whether or not something of the soul that bore it survives in these pages." Even when it was shown beyond a doubt, according to the statements of his contemporaries, that Swann was Haas, who could have determined whether this identity extended beyond the physical, social, or worldly appearance of these two figures? Proust stated, and I don't doubt him, that he had "filled" Haas "with a different kind of humanity"—none other than Proust's own.

A piece of scullery work that Françoise would well have appreciated ("by living with me, she had developed a kind of instinctive understanding of literary work, which was more accurate than that of many intelligent people, more carefully reasoned than that of many stupid people"). You may recall Françoise's fury in cutting the throat of the chicken, "looking at her enemy's corpse" while crying "Filthy animal! Filthy animal!" before a horrified Marcel, who would have liked to see "Françoise thrown out of the house immediately." By reinscribing Haas's death in his work, by carefully constructing his obituary in a fictional newspaper, Proust engaged in a culinary operation on Haas that Françoise would have been proud of, up to and including the sadism with which she executed her task. But Proust goes further: he kills the swan that has become a chicken, empties it, then stuffs it with another substance that he borrows from someone close by, so to speak, someone he knows well and who appears as plausibly novelesque as the creature he has just killed—Proust himself. (It is the verb "fill" that brought to mind the analogy between cooking and literature, together with the fact that Proust used it when he claimed that Haas was not Swann.)

In the cemetery of Père-Lachaise, where I was looking for Charles Haas's tomb, I—who never visit cemeteries—was surprised to see how many tombs there were whose names had been worn away. Moss had grown in their hollows, burying the letters that no amount of scratching would reveal, for time wears down, corrodes, and smooths the hardest stone. It is probably for this reason that men have replaced stones with books—small, portable, and reproducible urns.

The Frame and Its Canvas

THERE IS ANOTHER PASSAGE IN *IN SEARCH OF LOST TIME* IN WHICH Proust succumbs to what Robert Dreyfus referred to as his "enigmatic negligence," a point at which the novel leaves its moorings and sails into strange waters, where we no longer know—and apparently neither does Proust—whether what we are experiencing is literature or reality. Fortunately the passage seems to have been ignored by his august commentators.

A gradual loss of knowledge is the fate of successive generations. Whereas formal learning is transmitted from person to person and can grow with time, family secrets, considered trivial and inconsequential, fade away with barely a nod. The exception is the novelist, who "invents" the stories History did not judge worthy of preservation; he overcomes our defective memory and fills in the "blanks" for us. Robert de Saint-Loup, a Guermantes, and Gilberte de Forcheville, née Swann (shh!), had a daughter, Mademoiselle de Saint-Loup. Concerning this Saint-Loup, who, or so it seems, became something of a social misfit when she married "an obscure man of letters, for she was by no means a snob," Proust says that she "brought the family to a level lower than that from which it had started out." In other words we are led to believe that this family fell from the aristocracy to the bourgeoisie, indeed, that it had belonged to the aristocracy for all eternity. "It was then extremely difficult," wrote

Proust, "to convince the younger generations that their relatives in this obscure household had once had wealth and status." And then the lapse of logic: "The names of Swann and Odette de Crécy miraculously came back to life so that others could help you understand you were mistaken, that there was really nothing so remarkable about the family."

Exactly what sort of miracle has occurred here? How is it that the names of Swann and Odette de Crécy were able to come back to life to inform *us* about the upward and downward peregrinations of their family, one whose status is characterized by its belonging to fiction? And somehow, *miraculously*, it is Swann and Odette who were again talked about. Really talked about. Why? There can only be one reason: because I, Marcel Proust, have made them important characters in my books. And people have talked about them, about my books. (And of course Proust had received the Prix Goncourt for *Within a Budding Grove* in 1919, before this passage, which is found at the end of *Time Regained*, was written.) This is what rescued Swann and Odette from the oblivion that death, their fictional death as imaginary characters, had wrapped them in.

Proust occasionally treated his characters as if they were real people. It is not that the novel drifted into reality—Proust disliked naturalism—but something far worse: the book played with reality. It had real consequences. It informed reality. Was this sloppiness? Accident? The "enigmatic negligence" that Robert Dreyfus mentioned? Yes and no. Here naturalism is reversed and it is reality that looks to fiction for its sources. In other words, fiction has absorbed the real, emptying it of its substance, just as Proust did to the chicken/swan when he "reinfused" it with what I can't refuse myself the pleasure of calling madness.

Just as *Le Figaro* could write that a Valois had stepped out of his frame to give life to M. Charles Haas, Proust wrote that

M. Charles Haas had stepped out of the frame of Tissot's picture to give life to M. Charles Swann. It is Swann whom Proust addresses posthumously, asserting that people are still talking about him. The frame has burst into pieces.

The Hares of the Judengasse in Frankfurt am Main

At the beginning of the sixteenth century, there lived a certain Rabbi Meier, called the Red Rose, or *Roten Rose*, a native of Worms. His son, Slom (Salomon), lived in the Frankfurt ghetto (the *Judengasse*) in a house known as the Hare (*Haas*). He married a Miss Gutlin, the daughter of a Mr. Beer, also known as Boxwood (*Buchsbaum*), a native of Nuremberg. They had five sons. In the genealogy of the Jews of the German ghettos, the daughters are not taken into account, unless they are wives or daughters-in-law. This system, in spite of its obvious injustice, provides the great advantage of simplifying the recension.

The son of Slom the Hare who is of interest to our story is Samuel Hare I. He married a Miss Schönlin. They passed their time between the Hare residence and the Silver Crown (*Zilbernen Krone*). Samuel and Schönlin had two sons, one of whom, Samuel Hare II, lived in a house known as the Golden Crown (*Goldnen Krone*). He had three sons, one of whom, Salomon Hare II, also had a son, Model Hare, who lived in the house known as the Golden Hare (*Goldnen Haas*).

Model had a son, Salomon Model Hare, who married a Miss Léa Würzburg, daughter of Getz Würzburg. Salomon and Léa had three sons, one of whom, Getz Salomon, had two sons, one of whom was named Salomon Getz.

Salomon Getz had two sons, one of whom was Salomon Salomon. He married Esther Wetzlar, then Ella Kulp. Salomon Salomon and Ella had three sons, one of whom, Nathan Salomon Hare, was the paternal grandfather of our Charles.

Nathan Salomon died in 1802, leaving his wife, née Jette Franck, and a son, born on June 7, 1799. This son was named Antoine, which sounds neither Jewish nor German. He is our "Papa Swann," the stockbroker. He left for Paris following the Congress of Vienna in 1816 and moved into 9 rue d'Artois.

THE PARIS ARCHIVES prior to 1860 are located at the Hôtel de Saint-Aignan, 71 rue du Temple. (Later records are kept in a building on quai Henri IV.) An especially forbidding man greets visitors when they arrive at Saint-Aignan. He doesn't talk, he barks. Some people, coming here for the first time, or foreigners who speak French poorly, are extremely put off. I watched this intrepid character operate, for he was quite a character. Over and over he would repeat: "Birth, marriage, death? What are you looking for? Everything was burned here during the Commune. Nothing left! Here just for the day or you'll be back? Birth, marriage, death? What is it you're looking for? In any case nothing's left. . . . Take a table number. A table number! It doesn't matter anyway, everything burned, there's nothing left, the Commune . . . birth, marriage? What is it?"

But I was prepared. A woman from quai Henri IV had told me that at Saint-Aignan "they" were much less friendly than at "her" archives. Armed with this information I was quickly able to get past the Cerberus who served as the all-powerful master of the reading room. He wasn't such a bad egg. He was someone who took advantage of the little power he had (but it was sufficient to foul your well-tuned engine of desire for a while), turning his job as an obscure public servant into the screenplay for a film only Cecil B. De Mille could have made, a Cinema-Scope and stereo production on the life of galley slaves. The man was a congenital slave driver. My approach was to address him with as much polite humility as I could muster. Better still, I spoke to him as if he were my master. Suddenly he became quite easy to get along with. He told me what I needed to know. Showed me where to go. And later, when I was leaving the building, he even said good night to me. He's the nicest guy in the world. It's just that he's a bit gruff. The important thing was that I now had before me the marriage certificate for old Papa Haas.

> On Monday, March 22, 1824, Antoine Haas, 24 years of age, born in Frankfurt am Main on June 7, 1799, a teller at Rotschild [sic] brothers, bankers, residing at 9 rue d'Artois, Paris, the son, not yet of marriageable age, of Nathan Salomon Haas, shopkeeper, who passed away in Frankfurt on January 14, 1802, and Jette Franck, his widow and current wife of Meyer Speyer, wholesale merchant, residing in said Frankfurt, who has stated that he agrees to the marriage of said Antoine with Sophie Lan, 22 years of age, born in Paris on 11 Primaire, Year 10, corresponding to December 2, 1801, residing in Paris with her mother at 6 rue Saint-Merry, the daughter of Léon Lan, shopkeeper, who died in Rouen on January 8, 1823, and Jeannette Cerf Bodenheim, his widow, who is present and gives her consent. . . .
>
> Witnessed by: Sigismond Mannheim, 25 years of age, retail jeweler, friend of the groom; Jean-Marie Martin, 57 years of age, employee, friend of the bride; David Singer, 45 years of age, wholesaler, brother-in-law of the bride; Léopold Javal, 24 years of age, wholesaler, brother-in-law of the bride. . . .
>
> Madame Speyer has signed in German, having stated that she does not know French.

G. L. Landau, the archivist at the Jewish Consistory in Paris, called me. He had found a record for Antoine Haas, dated 1828, which I copied as he read to me over the phone:

Antoine Haas is among the fifty wealthiest Israelites in the Paris district. He lives at 26 rue Pinon. He is a teller for James de Rothschild. He is a foreigner. He is highly regarded.

I looked for rue Pinon in the Taride guide, as well as in the list of principal names of the streets of old Paris. There was no rue Pinon. G. Landau anticipated my question about the meaning of the term "teller." It should be understood as "Rothschild's right-hand man" rather than an ordinary bank clerk. Which is exactly how I had interpreted it.

1832 or 1833: birth of Charles Nathan Haas.

1837: Antoine requests, and obtains, his naturalization.

On this day, December 2, one thousand eight hundred thirty-seven, there came before me, the Deputy Mayor of the second arrondissement of Paris, M. Antoine Haas, property holder, born in Frankfurt am Main (a free city of Germany) on June 7, 1799, and currently residing at 21 rue Laffitte. Said M. Haas has stated that, having resided in France since 1816, he wishes to remain here and to make it his permanent home, there to enjoy his civil rights and obtain from His Majesty the favor of becoming a naturalized French citizen.

Antoine's signature followed:

What makes the signature so remarkable is that it appears to contain the name within two high walls that define some ineradicable *Judengasse*. What's more, the capital *A* in Antoine is considerably larger than the lowercase *h* in Haas and seems to insist on *Antoine*, as if to say: Today, I am French, and who would be so presumptuous as to claim the contrary? Finally, there are the two Hebrew letters that precede the name, *yudh* and *tsadik*. These are obviously to be read from right to left and constitute the initials of a Jewish first name, which could only be Itzhak, or Isaac.

Itzhak left the Jewish quarter of Frankfurt am Main in 1816 for the City of Lights and quite naturally changed his name to Antoine, just as Jakob the Red Shield (Rothschild) had become James, which was even better, or, as Odette would say, "smarter." Proust turned Haas into Swann by the same process of obliteration, this time not of his Jewishness—for this had been accomplished by the Christianization of the names Jakob and Itzhak—but of his Germanness, which amounted to the same thing at the time. The obliteration of Antoine's origins took place gradually, however. In his signature he retained the Hebrew letters of his original first name and used his father's name, Nathan, for the middle name of his second son, Charles.

Jakob the Red Shield (or Standard) and Itzhak Hare must have been on familiar terms. They came from the same ghetto in Frankfurt am Main, would live on the same rue Laffitte in Paris, Antoine at 21 and James at 15, in the town house he bought in 1818. But James's ambitions (and his means) were much greater than those of his fellow "countryman." He not only attempted to get elected to the prestigious Cercle de l'Union in 1829, he succeeded, taking great pride, it is said, in being the only member of his community to have done so. This brings to mind something else. Charles Haas wanted to imitate the banker for whom his father was a senior executive, and Charles himself was to become a member of the Paris Committee of the South Austrian Railway Company, a Rothschild company.

1838. Antoine had enjoyed his French citizenship for barely a year. He died on December 9, 1838, when Charles was seven years old. His mother, Sophie Lan, the widow Haas, remarried on February 18, 1845. Her second husband was a doctor, Mourgues Carrère, with whom she had a son, Gaston de Carrère. Gaston married the widow of a certain Comte de Loverdo, about whom I couldn't care less.

A Very Rarefied Elite

In *PAYS PARISIENS* (1932) DANIEL HALÉVY DESCRIBES THE TIGHT-knit world of his family friendships, a world that was later to become that of Charles Haas. It included Madame Hortense Howland, Albert Boulanger-Cavé, Edgar Degas, Jacques-Émile Blanche, de Vogüe, the Marquis du Lau, Madame de Broissia, Madame de Ludre. . . .

> It was a very rarified elite, one destined to serve from be-yond the grave. As for du Lau and those women I remember, they lived for friendship and only through their friendships.

A "Proustian" idea and one that Proust developed precisely on the occasion of Haas's death. It is those who are closest to us, our relatives and friends, who can attest to our existence. When you die they'll remember you and your name will be ut-tered from time to time. They will die in turn and that will be your true death. Your name will disappear from people's lips. This is much worse than a coin that has gone out of circula-tion. For the coin, an archaeological curiosity, might be discov-ered one day. But once your name has disappeared, it no longer represents anything. Once it has ceased to circulate, to pass from mouth to mouth, it will lose even its modest status as a memento. Or perhaps you will appear in photographs where you are seen talking with people, some summer afternoon, in a garden, on a beach, by a pool, and then one day you will no longer be there. Later, ten, perhaps twenty years later, . . . your very name will have been forgotten. These thoughts appear in Patrick Modiano's *Rue des boutiques obscures*. He calls us "beach people."

I imagine Haas and Swann as twins, or rather clones, walking down the *Boulevards* and wearing sandwich boards. On one would be written "We are all German Jews." On the other, "We are all beach people."

In my eyes Charles Haas (and I think Proust must have felt the same way) is the epitome of those beach people. I keep seeing a photograph that appeared in an American book, *The Proustian Community*. (I saw the book at the home of Bernadette A——, who bought a copy after I told her about it.) There is a bad photograph, gray, a bit fuzzy. The caption indicates that it was taken at Dieppe in 1880. The people in the photograph are seen in profile, straddling their chairs, which are aligned like the cars of a train. From left to right we see, again according to the caption, Robert de Montesquiou, Prince Edmond de Polignac, Charles Haas, and an unknown individual.

Their posture is striking. Equivocal. It's as if these men are strung together like those small colored beads on children's necklaces, each possessing a protrusion and an opening. I am particularly struck by the caption's reference to this "unknown" individual, a real "beach person." In 1880 everyone who was anyone knew him, spent time with him, enjoyed his company. His friends were important people. Today he is nothing more than an "unknown" and will probably remain so forever. In the end what does it matter?

I don't recognize Haas at all in this photograph. There is no indication of who the photographer was. I assume it was Ludovic Halévy.

We will all become "beach people" unless. . . . But let's hear what Daniel Halévy has to say:

Haas had a different and somewhat unique fate. Who would have believed this at the time, when everyone knew him to be a man of wit and sophistication who was determined to do nothing in life but remain a man of wit and sophistication? Charles Haas, although this was totally unforeseen at the time, entered into the realm of the illuminated. The Swann, the illustrious Swann, is our Haas.

Daniel Halévy can be taken at his word. He was intimately familiar with Haas and Proust, and *In Search of Lost Time.* I love his expression "our Haas." Imagine Halévy's astonishment when he suddenly discovered that the man he was friends with, although he was certainly interesting, cultivated, and refined, but not much more, was "famous." It's as if we were to learn that our best friend had won the Nobel Prize in literature when we were unaware he could even write. If we look for the signs that point forward to this unexpected destiny, we are certain to find them. Like Inspector Bourel of the TV series, we'll shout, "My God. Why of course!" This is exactly what Halévy did:

> The astonishing arc of his life had amused, interested Proust, and it's likely that he even envied him, making him the hero of his work.

That participle "amused" feels odd here, somehow improper. That this might have amused Halévy is understandable. It was amusing to watch this little man, this witty sophisticate, become the hero of such an immense and hugely admirable work. Amusing, yes. But that Haas might have "amused" Proust, that the arc of Haas's life had "amused" Proust, is extremely unlikely. He must have intrigued, fascinated, interested him, certainly, even if we use "interest" in its pejorative sense, for it was also out of *self-interest* that Proust took an interest in Haas. Yes, the "astonishing arc of his life" leaves no doubt that Proust felt envy, jealousy, even fascination when confronted with that life.

The American author of *The Proustian Community* (1971), Seth L. Wolitz, was correct when he wrote:

> Proust had evidence in the person of Charles Haas, the one Jew to enter the Jockey Club as well as being one of the most successful *mondains* of the age. Proust apparently wished to imitate his success. One could then say that Charles Haas was Proust's yardstick to social success in life as Swann is to the narrator in the work.

What efforts Haas made to achieve that success! Daniel Halévy writes, with visible admiration:

> Clearly, he succeeded admirably. So well, so perfectly, that when one was in the presence of Charles Haas, you forgot that you were watching him live the tour de force that was his life before you. A Jew from an obscure background, while still young he had set himself the goal of entering and becoming a part of the most closed society in the world, at a time when such societies actually existed. He had laid the groundwork for his plan as far back as 1860. The slow, careful, and intelligent maneuvers he must have planned have been forgotten. It was Proust, his creative genius, who made it all up.

But this can't be right. Genius, yes, certainly. But no, Proust didn't invent anything as far as Haas was concerned. Everything Halévy writes, exactly thirty years after Haas's death and twenty years after the appearance of *Swann's Way*, is exactly what Proust himself wrote, what Proust is supposed to have made up. He didn't invent all that much. And yet Proust barely knew Haas. He met him at most three times in his life and dared speak to him no more than once or twice at most. I imagine him engaging in polite, witty conversation: "What's that? You know the Comte de . . . , the Marquise de . . . ?" On the other hand Proust was aware of almost everything concerning the "astonishing arc of his life," to return to Daniel Halévy's telling expression. Was

Proust ever too tired to call a cab or write five long pages of a letter for the sole *self-interested* purpose—the higher and sacred cause of Art—of learning such details? "Tell me, is it true that certain people had such contempt for Haas that they would offer only their left hand to him?" Yes, in spite of his fatigue and illness, Proust had to have the answers to such anguished questions and he had to have them right away. Truly anguished. There were sleepless nights. The book was a nightmare.

It was with unfeigned admiration, a childlike admiration, that Daniel Halévy related the circumstances of Haas's admission to the Jockey Club. Fortunately, the recorder wasn't anti-Semitic. It's true that would have been difficult, but not impossible, and his description would certainly have taken a different turn.

> I recall hearing about the vaunted ease, along with a certain amount of luck of course, with which he managed to force his way into the Jockey, the first and last of his race to cross its threshold. He had turned the Paris siege to good account.

Some of the words Halévy uses are tinged with danger: "ease," "force his way into," "turned to good account." Especially at a time when the word "race," a presumably scientific term, was considered neutral. The mistake made is that Haas was not the first "of his race." Long before Haas, in 1852, Alphonse de Rothschild had been admitted. This brings to mind a line from Nietzsche, which struck me when I first read it:

> The profound contempt with which the Christian was treated in an ancient world that has retained its nobility can still be found today in the modern world's instinctive repulsion toward the Jews. It is the hatred of the free and self-conscious classes for those who manage to *insinuate themselves* and who combine timid gestures with an absurd sense of self.

The obscure Jew who has barely escaped the ghetto and attempts to achieve the highest possible social status in record time is a natural example of someone who *insinuates* himself. There is something illegitimate about his advancement. Clever, pushy, opportunistic. Depending on which side you're on, he is either an object of admiration—this was the case for Daniel Halévy and Proust—or anti-Semitic repulsion. This being said, it seems that Haas must have really *insinuated* himself, since he succeeded in "crossing the threshold" of the Jockey Club. It wasn't, as some would believe, including Proust, because of his bravery during the War of 1870 that he gained entrance into the Jockey Club, but pure historical opportunism, namely the siege of Paris.

Halévy put his finger on it when he wrote, "And what's more, to complete his success, Charles Haas has found his poet: Proust." As if Charles Haas had been put there for a purpose. There follows a curious remark by Halévy, which confirms the fact that he understood nothing about Haas: "What a shame that Proust didn't choose Cavé. . . ." No doubt Cavé was far more pleasant and sympathetic than Haas and certainly the Halévy family liked him a great deal. Daniel Halévy acknowledged the difference between the two men:

> Cavé was well known for having done nothing with his life. Nothing, absolutely nothing. This is extremely rare, and I'm wondering if he isn't unique. . . . Take Charles Haas, for example. He had the appearance and pretensions of an idler. But in truth his indolence was a mask that hid his ambition. There was an air of constant and exhausting preoccupation about him that affected his personality, which was somewhat artificial and tiring. "When traveling to Asnières, I prefer Haas," my father would say, "but if I'm traveling to Constantinople, I want Cavé." Degas remarked, "Haas is just so affected!"
>
> Similarly, du Lau was also rather indolent, but he had a single ambition, which was to serve his country.

All things considered, there was something "putrid" about

Haas, as Norpois is supposed to have remarked, according to Proust, about Swann.

I TELEPHONED DANIEL HALÉVY'S GRANDCHILDREN, Madame Yvan N———, whose mother, Madame Louis J———, Daniel's daughter, is elderly and possibly ill, and Jean-Pierre Halévy. There was a question of some photo albums that belonged to the family. Apparently, there were about ten photographs in which Haas, Proust, and Madame Straus appeared with the Halévy family at Sucy-en-Brie. Cousin A sent me to cousin B, cousin B to cousin A. Finally, cousin A assured me that she would call her cousin C at once to get the facts straight, since this was of interest to her as well. Apparently cousin C had disposed of dozens of Proust's letters without so much as telling the family. There was also a possibility that he had gotten rid of some photographs and would direct me back to her to avoid having to discuss the issue. I was unaware of any photo in which Proust and Haas appeared together. But Madame N——— insisted that not only did such a photograph exist, but also that it was very well known and could be seen everywhere in reproductions. It was as if someone had punched me in the stomach. I calmed down, began to dream about the photograph whose existence I had previously been unaware of, the very likelihood of whose existence I doubted. What I was most suspicious of was this intimacy between Proust and Haas. Proust's profound knowledge of Haas seemed to have its origin in comments made by a third party, either Geneviève Straus, Daniel Halévy, Robert de Montesquiou, the Prince de Polignac, or several other possible candidates.

With Jean-Pierre Halévy on the phone, we discussed Jacques Bizet. He told me that his grandfather held him in great esteem. Within the family the previous generation was reluctant to talk about the past, to transmit its knowledge; this meant that he had to rebuild everything from scratch, become a researcher of sorts. He reminded me of *Pays parisiens*, his grandfather's marvelous book, in which the names of du Lau, Madame Howland,

Cavé, and Haas are evoked, people who "lived for friendship and only through their friendships."

As soon as I hung up the phone, I rather mechanically picked up my notebook to look at the passages I had copied from Halévy's book. The following caught my eye:

> Madame Howland, Cavé, who, aside from myself, even remembers their names any longer? . . . Celebrity. . . . There are certain public arts that confer fame, even to mediocre individuals; their names can be found in catalogs. There are other arts, intimate and private, which they fail to report and which celebrity ignores.

As for Haas, Daniel Halévy continues, if it hadn't been for Proust. . . . Yes, that's exactly what Proust said. Because of me, Haas's name, excuse me, I mean Swann, survived and will continue to live on.

EARLIER I HAD CALLED Madame Louis J——, née Françoise Halévy. A personal companion, an aide, had referred me to her daughter, Claude, the wife of Yvan N——, the nephew, as I understood it, of a famous Russian American writer, and he to his cousin, Jean-Pierre. Which of the two had the photo albums of their great-grandfather, Ludovic Halévy? Each of them, Claude and Jean-Pierre, thought the other had it. They spoke to one another by phone. Madame Claude N—— called me back: I should get in touch with her other cousin, Dominique, the brother of Jean-Pierre, who had just returned from Africa. I called him at once. He referred me to his sister, Élisabeth R——.

I went to see her in Saint-Cloud, along the banks of the Seine. Seated side by side, we examined the album of old photographs, faded with time. It was a happy, tight-knit family, with lots of children, brothers, sisters, and cousins. There were gardens, many different gardens for many different homes: Sucy, Jouy. . . . Contentment, wealth, culture. How unlike my own memories! Several of the photographs were of Madame Straus and her only son, Jacques Bizet. I told Madame R—— that he had married Alice Sachs, the grandmother of Maurice Sachs, under rather dramatic circumstances that were very 1900. There were also pictures of Madame Howland, whom I had found so intriguing, as well as the chronically idle Albert Cavé. I asked Madame R—— if she would sketch the genealogical tree of the Halévy family, since I was unable to do it. She agreed, remarking that marriages in the family were sometimes between Catholics, sometimes between Protestants. She appeared to be quite satisfied with that arrangement. No doubt, in her eyes this was proof of the tolerance and openness of their social milieu. I was careful not to mention that, to me, Catholics, Protestants, Anglicans, Anabaptists, Jehovah's Witnesses, Mormons, Quakers, Maronites, and Seventh-Day Adventists were all the same, they were all goys. Élisabeth herself was preparing an exhibition on ecumenicalism. . . . What I didn't ask her was whether or not anyone in the family had ever married a Jew. Ultimately, I decided not to ask, fearing she would take it badly, would have been annoyed by the question, by its shocking impertinence, its incongruity, seeing it as a kind of betrayal. Still, it was strange that there was nothing, absolutely nothing Jewish about this family, whose name, Halévy, was almost a paradigm of Jewishness.

Élisabeth was indeed a charming woman. Friendly, intelligent, gifted with a sense of propriety, a good teacher. We discussed her "marvelous" grandfather, Daniel Halévy, from whom, she told me, each of the grandchildren claimed to have inherited a specific quality: Claude, Alain, "a highly secretive philosopher," Pierre, the current minister of the interior—Did she see him from time to time? Yes, at Christmas and New Year's, for birthdays—Denis. On the other side of the family there was Jean-Pierre, who, unlike Élisabeth, looked to the past, something she disapproved of, and Dominique. Obviously Daniel Halévy had a number of qualities, since there were plenty to go around. We discussed one of his books as well, one I was especially fond of, *Pays parisiens*. Later on, I, who did not have her education, her sense of propriety, and thus confirmed Proust's comment that in every Jew there lies a boor who looks for, and always succeeds in finding, opportunities to make his presence known, to break through the presentable but inauthentic facade, the way Napoleon broke through Bonaparte, almost against my will, made the blunder of mentioning Léonie Rodriguez, the wife of Fromental Halévy, who was supposed to have been mad. And his daughter, Geneviève Halévy, who had become Madame Bizet, then Madame Straus, and who had apparently suffered from "depression," a trait she had inherited from her mother. And her son, Jacques Bizet, a morphine-addicted invalid, whom Maurice Sachs had spoken so well of, but who committed suicide in 1922. And Émile Straus, who was supposedly a Rothschild "bastard." And. . . . But enough is enough. Élisabeth swept these rumors away with a gesture of her hand. Oh! She disapproved of them. I could see it on her face. I had hurt her, troubled her. And it was with some emotion that she finally remarked, "If we were to believe everything that's said. . . ." I decided not to pursue my boorishness any further.

LATER I THOUGHT about what had happened. It was clear enough. Because there was no trace of Haas to be found in what she had shown me, I was probably angry at Élisabeth—who couldn't have changed matters anyway—but still. . . . It was clear that she had nothing to tell me about Haas and in fact it was I who told her about him. I was the one who told her what she no doubt was unaware of, forced her to confront what she may have simply wished to ignore, namely, the mental illness which, according to rumor, had affected the other branch of the Halévy family, the Fromental side. I had convinced myself that she would enjoy knowing this. And since she apparently had nothing new to tell me and, consequently, I had no use for her, I could drive the nail in without remorse. I did this both to get back at her

for the fact that Haas was nowhere to be seen in the photographs and to discredit two aspects of her character (and
mine as well after all) that had irritated me: she had no use for
the past, didn't like to "stir up the past," as if doing so meant
stirring up the muck (which, frankly, is not far from my own
ideas on the matter, but then stirring up muck is something I
enjoy), and she exhibited a certain smooth and, to be blunt,
Christian exterior, Catholic to be precise, Marian, smooth and
white as a lily, impossibly smooth and white, like a virgin who
happened to be the mother of a family, possibly a grandmother.
But it was that first aspect that had hurt the most. To claim that
she had no use for the past (unlike her brother, Jean-Pierre) was
as if she had written me off from the start, had simply crossed
me out: Sir, I'm afraid we have nothing to say to one another.

Her husband was an amateur photographer. I was preparing
to leave when Élisabeth told me that he would make copies of
some of the pictures for me: Madame Straus, Jacques Bizet, et
cetera, but that she would wait until she had had a chance to
read what I had written before sending them.

EDGAR DEGAS. He was a strange character, Degas. He was very
close to the Halévy family, Ludovic and Louise, and their sons,
Élie and Daniel. The Dreyfus affair had added a bit of spice to
their friendship, especially on Ludovic's side. As for Daniel, he
never faltered in his esteem for the painter, never took his anti-
Semitism to heart. It's possible he chalked it all up to bad character—unyielding, disgruntled, misanthropic.

Degas and Haas met at the home of Madame Howland, a
"salon" woman. She had been a friend of Lamartine, and especially of Victor Cousin and Eugène Fromentin. Her correspondence with Fromentin served as the point of departure for *The
Masters of Past Time*. She was a friend of the Princesse Mathilde
and the Marquis du Lau as well. In *The Prisoner* Proust associates
du Lau with Madame Howland. At the end of her life, he
wrote, the Marquis du Lau, who was by then deaf, "had himself

carried to Madame H——, who was blind." It's strange that Proust limits himself to her initial, Madame H——. He had met her during the summer of 1893 at Saint-Moritz, with Robert de Montesquiou.

Hortense Colbert had married an American, Meredith Howland. In August 1895, she went to join him. Before embarking at Le Havre, she spent some time at Mont-Saint-Michel with Cavé and Degas. In any case, with Degas, for I'm almost certain that Cavé bowed out at the last moment. In August 1910, Daniel Halévy told Degas about Cavé's death. He reminded him of "Cavé, the lazy schemer and happy amateur," and a certain trip to Mont-Saint-Michel, where Cavé was prevented from going and about "Degas's anger at him and his final condemnation of the 'unenterprising Cavé.'" Daniel Halévy wrote about this in his *Journal.* That day, that day of August 1910, Degas supposedly told him, "Haas and Cavé are both dancers; they bow and scrape, but do nothing."

It seems that for Daniel Halévy and Degas, Cavé and Haas were interchangeable. It was only for Proust that their differences became significant. Haas was Jewish. His social success was certainly much greater, his amatory conquests legion. His last affair was both unexpected and scandalous and resulted in a daughter. Not Gilberte. There was, however, a difference of character: Haas's wit was somewhat more mannered, "affected," Degas said, that is—at least from the point of view of certain of his friends—a bit tiring.

A comment made by van Gogh about Degas helps explain his attitude toward Haas:

> Degas's painting is virile and impersonal precisely because he has accepted that he will be nothing more than a petty solicitor who wouldn't dream of letting himself go. He looks at those human animals who are stronger than he is, who f——k and f——k, and paints them well, precisely because he only pretends to f——k.

If Degas only "pretends to f——k," it's because the Jew f——ks for him. He's taken his place. And in doing so f——ks him, Degas. "They give it *all* to the Jewboys! The girls all want to ball the Jewboys. . . ." Degas was too refined to have written that. It's too "petty solicitor." The quotation is from Céline's *Bagatelles.*

During the summers of 1888 and 1889, Degas was taking the waters at Cauterets in the Pyrénées. He was being treated for respiratory illness by a certain Doctor Évariste Michel and stayed at both the Hôtel d'Angleterre and the Hôtel de France. In September 1888 he wrote to his friend, the sculptor Bartholomé: "The Baroness de P—— is here, one of Haas's former girlfriends. She was walking not long ago with Madame d'A——, another former girlfriend of Haas." Degas's fascination–repulsion for Haas is primarily sexual in nature. Within a few years anti-Semitism would be added to the mix. A sexually omnipotent Jew is, after all, intolerable.

The following summer, again at Cauterets, he wrote to Bartholomé:

> But I was about to deprive you of the pleasure of learning that Haas may arrive in eight or ten days, and that the attitude he assumes toward me—whether he acknowledges me or cuts me—may or may not cost him. He knows I don't give a damn about what others think. Does he have a plan and the courage to carry it out? You know how strange these ladies' men are with other men.

I am not unaware that, at the time, the verb "to cut someone" was roughly the equivalent of the modern verb "to snub" (both are found in Proust: in the *Search* "to cut someone" is one of the favorite expressions of Madame Swann, who was delighted to discover one day that "Madame Leroi 'had cut' the Marquise de Villeparisis"). So. The conjunction of parameters, Haas, the ladies' man (every woman that Degas runs into at the spa is a former "girlfriend of Haas") and Jew, ensure that Degas, who, according to van Gogh, "only pretends to f——k," would be terrified that if he were to run into Haas, he, that is Haas, would "cut," or castrate, him.

This did not prevent Degas, the following year, September 1890, from traveling with Haas from Pau to London (in the company of a certain Vicomte de Borelli). Haas's daughter, who was nine at the time, was in Lourdes, living with the nuns.

During the following summer—it was September 1891—he dined at Cavé's home with Madame Howland and Haas. He wrote to Ludovic Halévy, "Haas was *simple* and delicious as always." He underlined the word "simple." No doubt he was being ironic. But nothing is less certain. Proust also wrote that Swann was "very simple in his demeanor." If we never miss an opportunity to point out how simple someone is, clearly that person has every reason in the world to be otherwise.

And then there was the Affair. At first they watched one another, wondered how the others would react. They felt that suddenly things were unpredictable. Ludovic Halévy simply turned his back on the matter, played ostrich. He locked himself up in his office on rue de Douai, refused to sign the petitions that were circulating on behalf of the poor captain. As far as Cavé was concerned, the whole thing was a matter of considerable annoyance. "Thursdays" at rue de Douai risked going up in smoke, given the conflicting reactions of the guests. Degas, Émile Straus, and the others. Madame Howland, before deciding which side she was on, wanted to know where her friends stood. That meant Haas, of course, and Montesquiou, and those whom Jacques-Émile Blanche referred to as "the little chapel on rue La Rochefoucauld," which included Gustave Moreau, Ernest Reyer, the painter Élie Delaunay, and, of course, Degas.

But at this time Degas was mostly interested in photography. Toward the end of 1895 he took Daniel Halévy to see Classet, who made his prints for him: Mallarmé, Renoir, the Manet family, Madame Howland, to whom he refused to show her portrait. "She would feed it to her dog, that moron. The other day," he confided to Daniel Halévy, "I showed her my fine Haas. She said to me, 'He looks marbleized. You'll have to have him retouched.' What a moron! I didn't answer. I just looked at her, closed my package, and left." He had a quick temper, Degas. An artist. Toward the end of 1896, he made some enlargements, always the same people: Haas, Ernest Reyer, du Lau, Madame Howland. "He examined them with a childlike joy," remarked Daniel Halévy.

A child the Affair disturbed, mentally disturbed. There is a letter, unfortunately undated, to his friend Henri Rouart. Everything about this letter leads me to believe it was written about Haas:

> The poor Wandering Jew has just left us for good. He won't wander any longer, and if we had known, we would have walked behind him. What's been going on in his mind ever since this lousy *affair* began? What did he think about the fact that we couldn't help but feel uncomfortable in his presence? Did he ever say anything to you about it? I wonder what went on in that old Jewish head of his? Did he think he could simply go back to the time when we were more or less unaware of his awful race?

He relates a dream he had two days after having learned of the death of someone I assume to be Haas. He meets Haas in the dream and says to him, "But I thought you were dead!" Degas's comment, his denial of Haas's death, appears strongly self-contradictory, certainly in the context of his dream. So the poor Wandering Jew hasn't left yet! How annoying. He's still walking. His old Jewish head is still ticking. He makes everyone uncomfortable now that we know all about his awful background. It's a sad state of affairs, truly it is.

Degas's "old Jewish head" is hardly less cruel than Proust's remark about "Swann's punchinello nose . . . like that of an old Jew." Except that Proust deliberately sought, for a number of profound fictional reasons that affected the meaning of his work, to undo the hold that Swann had on the narrator of the work. In simply being himself, the potential writer he is, he must somehow participate in Swann's death, wish for it the way we wish for the death of a tutelary deity. Proust puts Swann to death after having degraded, vilified, soiled, and denigrated him—an intimation of the death to come—not without a certain element of sadism at the end, becoming Mademoiselle Vinteuil as she helps destroy her father. Yet Degas was purely and simply anti-Semitic, although his anti-Semitism was neither pure nor very simple. Take the expression "Wandering Jew" that Degas used. For Degas, any Jew ("He won't wander any longer . . .") is a Wandering Jew. The expression wasn't really so cruel, except for the fact that it was constantly used by Édouard Drumont as the equivalent of a Jew *tout court*, thus emphasizing his nomadic character. Quite by accident I found the following in *La Libre Parole* of July 26, 1893:

> Ever since the Wandering Jew has entered Parisian society, we have all become wanderers more or less. This season the French have been moving from one place to another without really knowing why. . . . From Trouville to Nice, they circulate for six months at a time. Nomadism has become the normal state of affairs for anyone with a home of their own. . . . Jews, of course, continue to lead the movement.

This was referred to as "the Wandering Jew does the spa." For Degas, going to Cauterets for the summer was the result of contamination by the Jews.

Music

From prince edmond de polignac to robert de montesquiou:

My Dear Robert,

Do you want to stop by to hear the King of Thule's Cup Quartet, which I often played for you at the Ludre home? It will be sung on Saturday evening (May 1) during the concert given by Madame Moitessier, Madame de Flavigny's mother, 42 rue d'Anjou.

As the author I am authorized to invite you and would be grateful if you were to take advantage of my offer. Charles Haas will be there; he's my second guest and a fan of the quartet.

For a prince to have lured a count with Haas's presence says a great deal about the enormous prestige he had in their eyes.

A word in passing about the Comtesse de Ludre. *Le Gaulois* of June 12, 1898, carried a report of her funeral services at the Church of Saint-Honoré-d'Eylau. Those present included the Ducs de Montmorency, de Bisaccia, d'Estissac, de Noailles, de Blacas, de Clermont-Tonnerre, and de Mouchy; Prince Murat and the Prince de Poix; the Marquis de Breteuil; Baron Alphonse de Rothschild; Comtesse Paul de Pourtalès; the Comte de Noailles; Comte Charles de Breteuil; the Marquis du

Lau; Comte Aimery de La Rochefoucauld; Monsieur Lavedan; and Monsieur Charles Haas.

In the society papers of the time, especially Arthur Meyer's paper (anti-Semitic detractors referred to Meyer as "a man in the fore"), such lists of participants at receptions and funerals were common. The name of Charles Haas could often be seen in these lists. Naturally, as befitting his station, he was always mentioned last.

Haas was a great friend of the musician-prince Edmond de Polignac. They had posed together for the Tissot painting, and it was at Polignac's home at 41 quai d'Orsay that Proust must have met Haas. Twice, three times at most. It was through Polignac as well that he conceived the idea for the "little phrase" in the sonata, which served as a Wagnerian leitmotiv and which Polignac invoked, that is, the notion of the recurring musical phrase, rather than Wagner, strictly speaking. In this circle Wagner was a great subject of conversation and the trip to Bayreuth was not merely a customary but a required social event, although it is unlikely that it reflected any real taste for his music.

Haas didn't like Wagner. From Munich he wrote a letter to Montesquiou, very Guermantes in spirit:

> I find the twilight of the gods to be a detestable work with nothing transcendent about it. The room was gloomy and complacent. In France this opera, which lasts seven hours here, wouldn't last ten minutes. Compared to this twilight, the Berlioz Requiem is a spirited waltz. Like Berrichon, I'm leaving for Switzerland. See you soon, dear poet!!!

Very Guermantes. In fact, very much like Verdurin with its patriotic connotations (Berlioz over Wagner, the French public better informed than the German, the use of upper case for the French work and its omission for the German), very much in keeping with the attitude of a German Jew who is not only no longer German but has converted. The comments of contemporary socialites, what they claim as their intimate and frank convictions, are equally devoid of authenticity. Either they repeat what they have just heard or, to demonstrate their "intellect," they assume a contrary position, trapped by their equally arbitrary use of paradox. As if they were breaking down an open door, they proclaim their truisms with such vehement sincerity that their listeners can only be impressed. Proust says the same thing in describing the Duchesse de Guermantes. She tells her cousin, the Comte d'Argencourt, that love is very mysterious, "with the intransigent conviction of a Wagnerian affirming to a clubman that *The Valkyrie* is more than just noise." To a clubman. . . . Can there be any question that Haas, in spite of his superior intellect, shared the political and aesthetic opinions of his fellow clubmen?

There is an incomplete and rather partisan comment by Élisabeth de Clermont-Tonnerre (who signed her work with her maiden name, É. de Gramont):

> Elegant and relaxed, Edmond de Polignac made a sharp contrast with Haas (Swann), that precious dandy. It's as if he had rehearsed before a mirror the gestures and remarks he would use during the evening.

As Élisabeth R———, the woman I met in Saint-Cloud, said to me: If we were to believe everything they say! In any event this confirms Degas's comment about Haas being affected. But Degas knew Haas quite well, unlike Madame de Gramont, who saw him, by her own admission, no more than once: "the parchmentlike skin stuck to a big Jewish nose, curly hair the color of pepper." It's Swann during the afternoon reception at the Prince de Guermantes's, his cheeks hollowed by illness, his nose "enormous," the nose "of an old Jew." Élisabeth de Gramont, although not on familiar terms with Haas/Swann, was admirably well informed about Proust. To the point that her reading of the *Search* and her recollection, her meager recollection of Haas, grew confused. In the end it was her memory of Swann alone that remained. Alternatively, Swann and Haas may have been as similar as twins. Daniel Halévy, who was very familiar with both of them, speaks of Haas in the same terms Proust uses to describe Swann. It is also significant that Élisabeth de Gramont, intentionally or otherwise, in *Robert de Montesquiou et Marcel Proust* (1925), momentarily stops calling Haas Haas. She imagines, in a way that would have been entirely reasonable, if it weren't for her confusion between the real and the fictional, a failed conversation, not between Haas and Proust, or between Swann and Marcel, but between Swann and Proust, losing herself on the same path of illogic that had led Proust himself astray:

> It is likely that the disdainful Swann was speaking over the head of the short young man without looking at him, the latter not daring to speak to him until twenty-five years later, "And yet, dear Charles Swann, whom I knew. . . ."

Yet she, Élisabeth de Gramont, surpasses Daniel Halévy elsewhere, when she speaks—an expert on the subject—of idleness, a sign of distinction at the time, *in illo tempore*, the mythic time of nostalgia:

> Gone today is that race of accomplished men, products of a life of absolute ease, which enabled them to become so deliciously blasé. Like Diplodocus, they disappeared, for lack of nourishment from a society regulated by the Taylor system.

The same regret is expressed by her in another work, *Au temps des équipages* (1928), about another place, Cannes, "before the arrival of the English." I ask the reader to forgive me for appearing to diverge slightly from my already erratic subject and running off like a hare through the underbrush, but the following passage is too good to pass up:

> At Cannes we were surrounded by indolence, even in the cadenced trot of the horses, which provided a rhythm for the nonchalance of the wintering beauties. . . . What re-

mains of that exciting time? Nothing. That past has died ten times over. It's not only the people who are dead, but their way of life, their way of dressing, thinking, feeling, speaking. A different humanity has replaced them. The gardens of Cannes are now buried in the past like the *Titanic* beneath the waves.

At the time of the Belle Époque, Haas may very well have longed for the splendor of the Second Empire, the Belle Époque's Belle Époque. After the Great War and with the arrival of the Roaring Twenties, one might have had reason to regret, along with Élisabeth de Gramont, the "nonchalance" and "excitement" of 1900. After the crisis of 1929, Maurice Sachs wasn't the only one to long for the madcap exuberance of the Paris of 1925. But once the Second World War had ended, as with Édith Piaf, there were no more regrets or, at most, a nostalgia for nostalgia. A time aptly described in some duchess's memoirs, which can be bought for fifty cents from any bookseller. And Proust. Yes, I almost forgot about him. Proust, who gave us his own *Titanic*, the *Titanic* he spent his life burying, sealed forever, concealed beneath the waves of his prose.

I was planning to speak about music. One day Madame de Gramont visited Frankfurt am Main, Antoine Haas's birthplace. Her sense of hearing was astonishingly musical, as the following "savory" passage demonstrates:

> Music is the noise of wealthy neighborhoods. The poor neighborhoods of Frankfurt replace it with strident cries in Juddish [*sic*]. . . . In it I rediscover the singsong intonations and prolonged whining of Jews who have yet to make their fortune.

What intrigues me about this quotation are the words "I rediscover." What could she possibly have rediscovered, this charming woman? What could she have known about those impoverished Jews and their whining?

The Sonata's Tale: Notes for a Learned Work That May Never Be Written

1. The unexpected appearance of the sonata during the soiree at Madame de Saint-Euverte's home. The sonata speaks. It speaks of Swann's former love and the degradation of his present love. It is this difference that gives birth to speech. (Modern linguists have confirmed this: in language all meaning is born of difference.) Yet, this difference came to nothing for Swann. In the past, speaking of his love, the little phrase said: it all amounts to nothing. Today, speaking of his anguish, it says: it all amounts to nothing. Where's the difference? Happiness, suffering. . . . Nothing more than the difference between two states that are identical in their shared insignificance. The sonata tells us that this difference is simultaneously the source of suffering and illusion, the vanity of that suffering. To love. To suffer. It is not the sonata's tale that is important but that the sonata speaks. All else is futile.

2. Swann is not Vinteuil. Proust knows this. But not Swann. Swann imagines in Vinteuil a suffering that is as great, if not greater, than his own. Surely the composer must have suffered greatly to conceive a piece of music so filled with suffering. However, and this is Proust's doing, Swann isn't fooled. Vinteuil did indeed suffer (because of his cherished but delinquent daughter). Swann, however, did not know this. By equalizing their supposedly shared suffering, Swann raised himself to the level of a great creative artist. He imagined himself to be Vinteuil. He thought it was enough to suffer.

3. Vinteuil was saved by his art. And Swann, through his identification with Vinteuil's art, was also saved. Swann was unaware of the fact that only Vinteuil had been saved. Not because he suffered—for suffering doesn't guarantee anything, it's an illusion, like love, or sex, or friendship—but because he had created something. It's true that Swann was saved by

Proust. I mean Haas. That is, Proust means Haas. And Haas alone. Haas alone was saved. He became Swann.

4. For Swann, on the other hand, there is no salvation, he is "lost." He died too soon to have known the septet and its sense of creative revelation. And even if he had known it, had known its "red and mysterious call," whose revealed truth, Proust says with vengeful cruelty, "would have been no use to him since the phrase may well have symbolized a call, but it could not have given him strength and made Swann the writer he never was."

5. Either you're a writer or you're not. One is born a writer. The feminine bearer of a receptacle within which echoes the necessary accident of a Call.

Revelry

A COLONEL IN THE FRENCH AFRICAN ARMY ADDED A NUMBER of refinements to what was known at the time as the "doe hunt." These events occurred during the Second Empire and the place was Fontainebleau. The celebrations began with a dinner served at Barbizon, in a painter's studio. Initially, the women had been handpicked from a number of Parisian brothels. It was subsequently judged wiser to replace them with individuals of higher social standing. They were given furs, dressed as deer, and sent into the forest. Once that was done, the horn was sounded, and the men took off in pursuit. There was one doe for every hunter. The same hunt, with its many variations, also took place in Saint-Cloud, Compiègne, and, apparently, even Paris. Maximilian of Austria, passing through the capital, wrote a letter to Franz Josef. The police intercepted the letter. "One has the impression that everything is so short lived," it read. Mérimée wrote, "It will last as long as it can."

Certain pleasures, however, took on a more cultural allure. In 1863—December 19, 1863, to be precise—the Duc de Mouchy presented one of the first musical variety shows ever to be seen: *Les Cascades de Mouchy*. This is what Robert Dreyfus was referring to in 1909 in his *Petite histoire de la revue de fin d'année*, which, by the simple fact that it made reference to Mouchy by name, had

Proust in tears. The author of this devastatingly dull "work of dramatic art" was the Marquis de Massa, a lieutenant of light infantry in Napoleon III's guards and official supplier to the imperial court. He was also one of the most sought-after society authors of the time. He had been—it is a small world—a classmate of Ludovic Halévy at the Collège Bourbon, which later became the Lycée Condorcet.

Two years later, in November 1865, the Marquis de Massa again turns up in Compiègne. The small, intimate theater of the imperial palace had been made available to him for the presentation of a two-act review, and the major scenes and the assignment of roles (thirty in all, including the extras) had been submitted to the empress. The play was called *Les Commentaires de César*, after the recently published work by Napoleon III, which was in all likelihood written by Mérimée. In the female roles: the Princesse de Metternich, the Comtesse de Pourtalès, the Marquise de Galliffet, the Baronne de Poilly, . . . all friends of Haas. In the male roles: the Marquis de Galliffet, the Vicomte de Fitz-James. The Prince de Metternich played piano, Viollet-le-Duc was the prompter. It lasted as long as it could. It went on for four years.

There were a number of "series" held in Compiègne. A series included between sixty and eighty people. There were two series of "series." The first consisted of "spoilsports," anyone who was straitlaced and boring. The second, the "elegant" series, included the Princesse de Metternich, the Comtesse de Pourtalès, the Marquise de Galliffet, the Baronne de Rothschild. Some people, and Haas was one of them, attended both "series." These included the Marquis de Massa, Colonel de Galliffet, the Vicomte de Fitz-James, the Princesse d'Essling (whom Haas stayed with in Nice shortly before his death), the Princesse Anna Murat, the Duchesse de Mouchy, the Duchesse de Morny. After the fall of the empire, the Marquis de Massa continued to produce his revues for the various Cercles. The participants were the same.

There is a very Second Empire side to Madame Verdurin. She dreams of "series." "I wonder if, rather than trying to unsuccessfully blend people together, I shouldn't have a series just for boring people, so that I could really enjoy my little circle." The concerns of Madame V——.

But to return to the animals. A famous "animal ball" was given by the Princesse de Sagan (disrespectful Françoise called her *la Sagante*) in the Villa Persane at Trouville, in May 1885. Haas honored the occasion with his presence. Bumblebees and honeybees. The following appeared in *Le Gaulois:*

> Rising at daybreak, the bumblebees fly around the hive, which they regard with the careful eye of connoisseurs standing before a masterpiece. The honeybees, whom the rose-fingered dawn has drawn out of the hive, approach the gallant bumblebees, and after taking flight, bumblebees and honeybees join ranks. The queen bee (the Comtesse de Gontaud) chooses a king. Comte Jean de Beaumont turns out to be the lucky bee (choreographically speaking) and the couple takes flight, swirling round and round in the midst of the other dancers.

An indignant Drumont wrote in *La France juive* (where, I admit, I'm reading these lines), "Of course, every Jew in the city was there, laughing at the self-debasement of this ill-fated aristocracy." Neither Drumont nor *Le Gaulois* clarifies whether Haas was in disguise or whether he was there only as an aesthete or, more accurately, as a voyeur. I have a hard time imagining Swann dressed as a fat bumblebee, beating his wings in mad pursuit of his queen. But who knows? In his fascination with the *gentry* he may have gone to such lengths.

A number of Haas's friends were present at the ball:

the Vicomte and Vicomtesse de Turenne

the Comte and Comtesse de Vogüe (the comtesse appeared as a bird of paradise) the Comte and Comtesse de Rosa de Fitz-James (The comtesse, a Viennese Jew whose maiden name was Gutmann, held a salon that was frequented by the German philosopher Keyserling, Paul Bourget, the abbé Mugnier, the Comte de Turenne, and Haas.)

the Comte and Comtesse Aimery de La Rochefoucauld (the comtesse as a honeybee)

the Duc and Duchesse de Bisaccia

the Comte and Comtesse de Saint-Gilles (In the manuscript department of the Bibliothèque Nationale, I came across a telegram dated June 1894 that had been sent by the Comtesse Edmond de Pourtalès to Robert de Montesquiou. "I would very much like to see you so that I can prepare my list with you. The Saint-Gilleses and Monsieur Haas are, naturally, on the list. Would you like to come Monday around two with the young man? He'll try out my piano while we talk. I don't want to invite more than a hundred and fifty people at the most the most [sic].")

the Marquise de Galliffet (a honeybee)

the inevitable Marquis de Massa

the Comte de Brissac

the Comte François de Gontaud (He formed the front half of a giraffe, demonstrating, first, that Hymenoptera were not the only creatures present and, second, that there must have been another half of giraffe, at least for the sake of aesthetic integrity. And in fact . . .)

his brother (formed the back half)

the Comtesse de Blacas (a chicken)

the Baronne Gustave de Rothschild (a bat)

Madame Lambert-Rothschild (a panther: She wore a skirt of blue tulle decorated with gold beads and fine pearls, with a bodice and train of brocaded velvet in an imitation-panther-skin pattern, which covered the rear of the skirt and ended in a Louis XIII lambrequin. Her hair was crowned with a panther head that was held in place by a diamond crescent.)

AT MIDNIGHT A DRUMROLL sounded. The ballet began. A swarm of bees rushed from an enormous hive. Drumont concludes: "This is how Christians occupied themselves in the month of May 1885, to celebrate the profanation of the Church of Saint-Geneviève! . . . All this just to get a mention in Arthur Meyer's newspaper! This Meyer is the real master of Parisian society, the arbiter of all taste, the man behind all the celebrations. These Jews have never produced so successful an individual."

Arthur Meyer was a close friend of Charles Haas. It was Meyer who introduced him to Rosine Bernard, by then known as Sarah Bernhardt. The only one of the three, notwithstanding the Jewish names she chose for herself, who wasn't Jewish. Why, at this moment in time, precisely at this moment, would an actress intent on making a career for herself come up with the idea—a brilliant idea perhaps—of calling herself Sarah Bernhardt? Proust was certainly unaware that Haas and Sarah were lovers, for I don't see how he would have failed to point this out. Or was it simply too good to be true?

The Affair

Wʜᴇɴ ᴀsᴋᴇᴅ ʙʏ ʙʟᴏᴄʜ, sᴡᴀɴɴ ʀᴇғᴜsᴇᴅ ᴛᴏ ᴀᴅᴅ ʜɪs ɴᴀᴍᴇ ᴛᴏ the list of signatures in support of Picquart. Even though Swann was a Dreyfusard. He said, "I would very much like to live long enough to see Dreyfus rehabilitated and Picquart a colonel." Proust offered two reasons for his reticence. The first is somewhat incredulous: Swann found his name to be "too Hebraic not to have a negative impact." The second was more plausible. He did not want "to get mixed up in any way in an antimilitarist campaign."

> Swann refused to sign Bloch's petition, so that, even though many thought he was a wild-eyed Dreyfusard, my comrade found him tepid, infected with nationalism, and a chauvinist.

Yet Swann was a passionate Dreyfusard, and in this his sense of judgment was clouded. As soon as he learns that Saint-Loup is on his side, his esteem for the man grows. The same for his literary taste, which was also reversed. Barrès was now worthless. Clemenceau became a first-rate writer. There were similar inanities among the anti-Dreyfusards, for whom anyone who defended the captain was inevitably of Jewish origin. The argument carried, however, for Swann seems to have been aware of it. And it was precisely to avoid making himself an easy target for such critics that he refused to add his "too Hebraic" name to Bloch's petition. This might have been perfectly reasonable except for one small detail that immediately jumps out at the reader, like the "purloined letter" to Dupin: there is nothing remotely "Hebraic" about Swann's name. It is English. It is *not even* German. As a reason for refusing to sign his name, Swann's argument is simply absurd.

The only one this would have made sense for was Haas. And in fact Haas did refuse to sign the petition for that very reason. Here too Proust confuses Charles Haas and Charles Swann. Simple common sense should have prevented him from writing about the swan what could only have been written about the hare. I keep asking myself throughout this book—and, most likely, will continue to do so long afterward—why I find this "non sequitur" to be magnificent.

But I had to know for sure. Was Haas a Dreyfusard or not? After all, I had no idea one way or the other. And several factors led me to believe, to suspect just the opposite: (1) He had converted and therefore abandoned any sense of union with other Jews. (2) His friends at the Jockey Club were notoriously ultra-conservative and therefore anti-Dreyfusard. (3) His friend Arthur Meyer, the managing director of *Le Gaulois,* was a Jew who not only agitated against the captain but also contributed financially to the support of Colonel Henry, who forged the document used to convict Dreyfus. An anti-Semitic Jew, an easy target for anti-Semites, a paradoxical irony, although not so surprising as it might seem. (4) He provided his daughter, Luisita, with the most Catholic education possible. Ultimately, I felt it was simply a matter of cowardice or, at least, confusion. To have believed so intently in France and its values and suddenly watch them trampled under foot must leave you with a feeling of bitterness and dejection. And yet I had to partially absolve him since most Jews, at the beginning of the Affair, would have reacted with silence and discomfort. What's more, I said to myself, Haas wasn't an "intellectual," as the word was beginning to be used at the time. He had nothing to do with the École Normale Supérieure, which was populated by the first partisans of revision. He was certainly not an artist. No, Haas was nothing but a socialite, a dandy, a snob. Yet sometimes, this character. . . . I suddenly understood one of the reasons why Proust, that is, the narrator, one day detached himself from the character of Swann, how, perhaps, just as Odette simply stopped being for Swann the exclusive object of his passion, desire, and suffering, and disappeared from Swann's mind the way a symptom suddenly disappears from a sick man who has been healed, how one day all the signs had, mysteriously, suddenly fallen away from Swann, all the attributes of prestige the narrator had so long seen in him.

> I was unable to understand how I had once been able to surround that excellent, cultivated man, whom I certainly didn't regret meeting, with such a sense of mystery that his appearance on the Champs-Élysées made my heart race so fast that I was embarrassed to approach his silk-lined cape . . . all that had vanished, not only from his home, but from the man himself.

He was not an "intellectual." Not in the combative sense understood in the 1890s nor in today's sense. His aesthetic tastes, for example. Charles Haas did not like the modern art of his time, unlike another Charles, whom Proust scholars have advanced as a possible "model" for Swann, Charles Ephrussi, the managing director of *La Gazette des Beaux-Arts.* Haas detested Renoir and disliked Wagner (yet he traveled to Bayreuth). He preferred Montesquiou to other poets and Edmond de Polignac to other composers. His aesthetic tastes were governed by his man-about-town's sense of social instinct.

But what about Dreyfus? I went to the department of manuscripts at the Bibliothèque Nationale. Before arriving at the bus stop on the broad *Boulevards* that would take me to rue de Richelieu, I passed a newsstand near Porte Saint-Denis, where the owner had on display a photocopy of a page from *France-Soir,* the illustration of a horrible crime. Obviously I was not in as much of a hurry to get to the library as I had thought. Looking back, I realize that when I arrived, I was afraid even to approach the library and that my fear was as intense as the fear that would have accompanied the imminent, and unwanted, discovery of a truth about myself. My fear was either that I would find nothing to satisfy my question—and any police inspector (or writer) knows how demoralizing it can be to go through so much trouble only to end up with nothing—or that I would, on the contrary, find the information, but it would be the opposite of what I had hoped for, suddenly and pitilessly destroying the elegant hypotheses I had constructed. So I hesitated at the newsstand in front of the page from *France-Soir*.

The event took place in Germany. A four-year-old boy had been found in a room, naked. He was alive but covered with excrement and bits of food. The child was unable to speak. He barked, his mother being the dog who had adopted him as her pup. When his rescuers tried to approach the child, the dog growled and bared her teeth. The child would spend his days curled up against the dog's warmth. He slept on his stomach, his head beneath his "paws." With his "mother" he would gnaw on old bones. The child's face was surprisingly clean—the police had noted that the dog would lick him from time to time. It was the child's grandmother who told the police what had happened. But after four years of silence. Why the delay? No one knew. The neighbors had noticed nothing unusual, except that sometimes the child would look wistfully out the window, the dog's large head beside him.

A sidebar on the same page reported Alain Delon's reaction to the event. He said he was scandalized and was prepared to adopt the dog and, once the child had been treated and educated in a special institution, he would return her to him (or him to her). In Germany they were prepared to sell the dog to the actor. Ten thousand francs. Delon could certainly afford to pay, but found the request outrageous. . . .

AT THE B.N. there were letters from Haas to Comte Robert de Montesquiou. (In the *Search* he is often familiarly referred to as *Quiou*. The Duchesse de Guermantes is doubly familiar. She calls him *Quiou-Quiou*.)

Platitudes, preciosity. Haas wrote to Quiou using his own (Quiou's) style. The following two examples are proof enough. The first letter refers to a work by the comte, *Le Chef des odeurs suaves:*

TO THE MASTER OF SUAVE FRAGRANCES
———— o ————

Poet-chevalier because the so lovely Muse
Dreamer made you dream in the shadow of the fig tree
Under whose green canopy she frolics and plays;
The Man has become Master and the tree the schoolboy.

                                    Ficus ruminalis

From the 🖋 to the Sky **8** for the star
Earth

                                    Strength-Power-Authority!

The second refers to another book, *Félicité*, which the poet had sent to him:

> I received this admirable morsel and want to thank you for sending it. *History* will not overlook this document, this monument, this *testament* of our age. . . . For History will never surpass it.

A comment by Gustave Khan, the inventor, along with Jules Laforgue, of free verse, seemed somewhat more consistent with the mainstream: "How is it that his nullity irritates us so much more than other nullities?" he wrote of Montesquiou in *La Revue blanche*. "Because it is more profound? No, because it is more mannered. It's a culture medium for growing microbes of frivolity."

But I wanted, I think, to speak about the Affair. What is certain is that the Affair reminded Haas that he was Jewish. In this sense the personal destinies of Haas and Swann are completely parallel, including their complexity and the underlying complications. Both men died "good" Christians. Funeral ceremonies for Haas were held at Saint-François-de-Sales in Paris, Swann's in the church at Combray. Therefore Proust was stretching things a bit when he wrote that Swann had "returned to the religious cradle of his elders." Swann had become a Jew once more, Proust says it again. But "religious cradle," no. That wasn't quite it. Which is why the situation is not as simple as it might appear. Not for Haas and not for Swann. The error, or at least the contradiction, can't be blamed on Proust, however. The error, or contradiction, involved in becoming a Jew again at the very moment Swann/Haas is wracked by a fatal disease that will ultimately destroy him and see him die a Christian is like the wandering of those Israelites whom the Affair struck with the force of an earthquake, destroying the dwelling they had anticipated after so many centuries spent living in exile, in ghettos, and in forced exclusion. So Swann/Haas, under duress, again becomes a Jew:

> There are in certain Israelites—although extremely sophisticated and refined men of the world—in whom they remain in reserve, in the wings, waiting for the moment when they can make an entrance into their life, as in a play, a boor and a prophet. Swann had reached the age of the prophet.

Let us cross, with alert and careful step, the little bridge where, for better or worse, boor and prophet buttress one another, and examine the factors that might explain Swann's return not to the religious but simply the personal (or "ethnic") "cradle" of his ancestors. Proust gives us three factors: "grafted to one another, the fatal disease, the Dreyfus affair, anti-Semitic propaganda." Swann awakens to a sense of Jewishness that he seems always to have overlooked and that yet persisted as an imperceptible trace. This is reflected in the fragile association of ideas found in

Proust. Not even a metaphor, simply a banal comparison, without any significant justification, unless one knows how to read the expression: a faint trace of Jewishness. In the Swanns' apartment there is "an enormous coatrack with seven branches," writes Proust, "like the candelabrum found in scripture." Not much of a residue.

THE HANDFUL OF LETTERS from Haas to Joseph Reinach (6 avenue Van-Dyck), which I laboriously attempted to decipher in the manuscripts department of the Bibliothèque Nationale, were further evidence of his Dreyfusism. It wasn't for nothing that Proust spoke of the "prophet" who late in life had awakened in Swann. The problem remained, however, that in the *Search*, there was nothing to provide a content, a justification for this expression, which ultimately remained strangely devoid of meaning. Did Proust want to say that there was something of the prophet about Swann, as a Dreyfusard, fighting for truth and justice? There seems little justification for it. Bloch, who was far more committed, and an intense activist, was much worthier of the title. Otherwise, the word "prophet" had to be read as a mystical equivalent of what Péguy, in *Temporal and Eternal* (1910), called a "hero." "We were heroes. It must be said very simply, for I certainly don't believe that anyone is going to say it for us." Péguy was the man for whom the Dreyfus affair was "an essentially mystical affair." But Swann is in no way and at no time "heroic" in Proust. On the contrary, he is so cautious that Bloch found him "tepid, infected with nationalism, and chauvinistic." Not very prophetic, and not at all a mystic "hero" as in Péguy. No, there is nothing in Swann that can supply a content for this "prophet." For example, it is hard to take much satisfaction in the sudden and belated emergence of his Jewish nose, now thrown into prominence by his cheeks, sunken from disease, as a critical sign that would have indicated the growth of a strong feeling of Jewishness. A prophet's nose is not much to go by. Even a prophet's nose, since it is clear that it refers to the trivially well known "big Jewish nose." And yet, yes, Proust knows what he's talking about. He really did ask everyone. He was very familiar with *his* Haas. And he is indeed referring to Haas.

> Dear Sir, your letter did me good and I share your hope, but let's bear in mind what you said one evening at the Strauss's home [*sic*].

(In Madame Verdurin's pro-Dreyfus salon were assembled Picquart, Clemenceau, Zola, Reinach, Labori. . . .)

> "This will inevitably backfire when the truth is out. I have faith in the love of justice, in the native generosity of the French . . ." and your optimism astonished Madame Strauss [*sic*] and me. . . . Alongside this factitious and violent anti-Semitism, there has been, there will always be, the traditional anti-Semitism that traces its lineage to Judas. . . . Dreyfus's legend obliterates the legend of Judas, and in this amazing revelation you may have the leading role. . . . But, dear sir, France has yet to be converted. Persuade this nation of unthinking Women of the evidence.

Yes, Dreyfus's legend obliterates the legend of Judas. It's aptly put, although somewhat optimistic. But I am less fond of "this nation of unthinking Women." An astonishing remark coming from this "lady's man," as Degas called him. Or maybe not, perhaps not so astonishing. But I must be careful that I do not, like the painter, experience that sense of jealous resentment toward a man who had them all.

> So now the general staff has been revealed for what it is. How? By a group of dishonorable officers, a list of whose names would be easy to prepare. He destroyed himself like Henry and like everything else that becomes part of history—governments, institutions, individuals. Let us humble ourselves so we can better demonstrate that he is the one true architect of his fall and shout: Long live the new army!

There's still something unclear in this story. According to this letter from Haas to Reinach, in which he calls for a reform of the army, Haas should have been delighted with the appointment by Waldeck-Rousseau of his friend Galliffet to the War Ministry and with his efforts to overhaul it. Not at all. I read in Painter that Haas sided with the Marquis du Lau and other nationalist members of the Jockey Club in "cutting" General Galliffet.

But after all, Charles Swann's situation wasn't much clearer. He is both a Dreyfusard and, according to Bloch, "infected with nationalism." It was for this that he began wearing "something he had never done before, the decoration he had been awarded as a young recruit in '70, and he added a codicil to his will, asking that, contrary to his earlier request, he be given military honors appropriate to his rank as a Chevalier of the Legion of Honor."

Yet, in continuing the letter to Joseph Reinach, another, and highly "political," motive appears. If Haas shouts, "Long live the new army!" it's not so much for the honor of the army itself but because the expression cancelled ipso facto any suspicion that he may have had other motives, possibly associated with the "syndicate," with "Jews." With his "Long live the new army!" Haas remained within exclusively republican, even patriotic, limits.

> I'm not sure if the expression is appropriate, but what is
> important is that the triumph of Israel not be apparent.

There is a similar sense of remarkable political acumen in both Swann and Haas. And for good reason.

Like the vast majority of the Jewish bourgeoisie of his time, Swann/Haas was a true patriot, and there was nothing affected about his patriotism. (There was an intellectual fringe that, as a result of the Dreyfus affair—and because of the affair—became nascent Zionists. This group included Bernard Lazare, whom Péguy, rightly, refers to as a "prophet.") If Haas is horrified by anti-Semitic persecution, it is not so much because of the harm done to Jews but the catastrophic consequences that might be in store for France. In this, all mysticism aside, he is much closer to Péguy (who is concerned about the "eternal safety of France") than to Bernard Lazare.

> I am surrounded by imbeciles or, rather, by people who are still terrorized, with whom it is impossible to speak about the affair! For example, to whom could I explain that persecution might turn out badly?

Reading these words, I thought I heard an echo of the narrator's annoyance (and also my own with respect to Haas) when he exclaims, "Since Swann complains so much of being 'surrounded by imbeciles,' why does he continue to see them?" Jews of that time were most inclined to treat the Dreyfus affair, anti-Semitism, and so forth, as especially damaging for France. It was as if, all things being equal, a German Jew, living while Hitler was in power, were to believe that anti-Semitic persecution was dangerous . . . for Germany! *Deutschland über Alles! Vive la France!* Long live the new army! For this was precisely what Haas feared—that French Jews would become expatriates. And he used the word "exodus," meaning that modern France would become ancient Egypt. As for the land of Canaan, it was England:

> It's true that the Jews love France the way Heine—a German!—did, but patience has its limits . . . and England opens its arms to them. This year the Prince of Wales made very demonstrative advances toward a Jewish woman of my acquaintance.

And if Haas feared a Jewish exodus from France to England, it was because, being a patriot, this would have strengthened Albion.

> England's power would be compounded by the power of Israel. I think France would have reason to repent. For Zion is indeed London!!

However, a second letter to Joseph Reinach demonstrates that Haas's attachment to France has been deeply shaken. He certainly has not crossed the threshold to Zionism, but he has gone much further than his correspondent. For Haas the Affair served as a cataclysmic event that split the Jew from the Frenchman. Now, there was a before and an after for Haas.

> One of my friends, a woman, shared a conversation she had had with one of her woman friends, in which this friend spoke to her of the great danger posed by the presence of Jewish officers in the army. That was the watchword; the only thing missing was for the right moment to arrive. I answered that this was absurd, that if the Jews had a homeland, it was France, that other homeland . . . how naive I was. . . . I find in you a sublime form of that same naïveté. You still believe in the revolution and in France, in spite of everything, and if anyone is genuinely patriotic, it's you! For France and the revolution are Saint Bartholomew and '93!! You too are a republican in this republic, which has abandoned us because we took it seriously.

No doubt "prophet" is a bit excessive. Initially Haas was a Dreyfusard, but his support was circumscribed within the limits of a sincere patriotism. Like Péguy he seems to have been most concerned about the "safety" of France, even though he would have given the term a very different meaning, not at all mystical but political. Subsequently, his patriotism was shaken. The history of France is not without its stains: the wars of religion, the Terror, the anti-Semitism exposed by the Affair. . . . When he writes to Reinach, "You too are a republican in this republic, which has abandoned us because we took it seriously," and in doing so appears to make a clean break with him, first, who is this "us" who is so clearly unrelated to his interlocutor? This could only be—us Jews. This "us" is something I can't imagine Swann ever saying. For Swann (speaking with Bloch and the narrator, and joking, jibing, as if there were something in their impromptu meeting that he found compromising and discomfiting), this "us" could only be political. It was the universal "us" of the Dreyfusards rather than the ethnic "us."

Is the sense of despair transitory for Haas, associated with a moment of unusual confusion? We don't know. It seems that, although equally lucid, Haas is simply somewhat more pessimistic than Swann. Yet the difference is just a matter of degree. Swann: "I admit that it would be distressing to die before the end of the Dreyfus affair. Those scoundrels have more than one trick up their sleeve. . . . I would like to live long enough to see Dreyfus reinstated and Picquart a colonel." Swann is an optimist. It's as if he had said, I would at least like to live until Christmas, or Easter. But whether he lives or dies, Christmas and Easter will arrive. The captain's reinstatement and Picquart's promotion are, however, events that can't be predicted . . . except by a prophet. This prediction is largely based on the fact that Proust knew the outcome of the Affair. As for Haas, he had his nose pressed against the window of the Affair; for him it was breaking news.

> How will this be retried? With whom? With other officers? Before an unreformed court-martial? That is, without any new judicial elements? With other officers who are waiting to take revenge for the first court-martial? Orders will have nothing to do with their judgments, rancor will be enough.

These letters, which I had been so reluctant to read, completely reconciled me to my character, who had once appeared so distant. He was no longer the frivolous and conceited socialite I thought he was but a lucid, and broken, man. "Having arrived prematurely at the end of his life, like an exhausted animal brought to ground, he cursed these persecutions."

A Grand Story

GALLIFFET. THE NAME IS DERIVED FROM *GALLUS FACTUS:* "MADE A Gaul." In other words, a Jew who converted to Christianity. Or was discredited, like Galliffet. In March 1871, on Thiers's orders, he took the fort of Châtillon, with the assistance of another old friend of Haas, the Marquis du Lau, who was then a captain but was to become a major. There is a story that Proust, while visiting the Louvre, stopped before Ghirlandaio's painting of the old man and the child and exclaimed "That's the spitting image of Monsieur du Lau!" This was one of Swann's obsessions. There's no reason why it should be associated with Haas, though, this obsession. Haas, Proust told Gabriel Astruc, who recognized him in Swann, was "filled by me with a different humanity." But Proust did not have to go far to find this different humanity in which Swann *is not* Haas: he found it in himself.

(Gilberte, after the death of her father, was for some reason ashamed to be recognized as Swann's daughter yet curious about everything that related to him. She asked the Duchesse de Guermantes about Monsieur du Lau. The laconic duchess told her he was ill and confined to his home, then quickly changed the subject, leaving Gilberte's curiosity unsatisfied.)

Two months later, in May, Galliffet was the commanding officer when the Communards were shot down. That evening, along with his general staff, he had a quiet dinner at the Jockey Club. I wonder if Haas was at that dinner. He had been a member of the club since January.

Galliffet quit the Jockey Club the following year, although he continued to frequent the Cercle de l'Union. After all, the Jockey's members, as conservative as they were, didn't necessarily have a taste for military slaughter. Much later, Galliffet, now a general, was appointed to the Waldeck-Rousseau cabinet as minister of war. He was responsible for reforming the army, cleaning it up, and plugging any leaks. His friends in the Cercle de l'Union were now a source of embarrassment for Galliffet, so he quit. The Duc de Rohan, president, approved his resignation. "All the members of the Cercle being opposed to the government of which you are a member, it seems natural that you have decided to resign your membership." As a "revisionist," he had become hated by the right for having served as a witness on behalf of Lieutenant Colonel Picquart. He didn't fare much better with the left. Upon entering the Chamber of Deputies, Galliffet was greeted by cries of "Assassin!" "Assassin!" from leftist politicians. Poor Galliffet.

Haas, du Lau, and Galliffet were often seen at the Café Anglais, on the *Grands Boulevards* of Paris. According to the novelist Karen Blixen, Galliffet once sat next to a certain fictional General Löwenhielm. On the menu were "quails in a sarcophagus," a creation of the head chef at the Café Anglais, the no less fictional Babette Hersant, the central character in Blixen's novel. During the Commune, her husband and son were killed and Babette herself was arrested for being an "arsonist." She immigrated to Berlewaag, Norway, in June 1871, with a letter of recommendation from the musician Achille Papin, addressed to two old maids living in a small Puritan community. Galliffet so appreciated Babette's cooking that he said she was the only woman for whom he would again risk his life. What I failed to understand, when reading lovely Karen Blixen's *Babette's Feast*, lovely simply because I imagine her looking like Meryl Streep in *Out of Africa*, is why the young woman had to go into exile. Wouldn't Galliffet have spared her, arsonist that she was, for her artistry in preparing quail?

Painter says that Haas was a faithful customer of "old Isabelle," who used to sell flowers every evening by the door of the Café Anglais. How did Painter learn about Isabelle, the old flower vendor? This was yet another of those painfully acute questions with which my life was filled. I learned that in 1857 Isabelle had been appointed "Flower Girl of the Jockey Club," thus obtaining the monopoly for selling flowers to its members. It was one of the founders, Ernest Le Roy, who suggested her for the position.

Within the Café Anglais was a special room, known as the *Grand Seize*. I can imagine the kind of events that must have taken place there. But I'm only imagining. Haas also frequented Paillard, the restaurant where the manager of the Grand Hôtel de Balbec cut his teeth. On certain evenings the Prince of Wales and the Marquis du Lau could be found there, along with several female companions.

Édith Piaf's grandmother was a madam in a brothel known as "Le Grand Seize" in the town of Bernay, in the Eure region of France. Does the number have any significance? (I read this one sunny Sunday in autumn in the Buttes-Chaumont, where we had taken our daughter, who had gone, alone, to the open-air puppet show. While she watched the show, we walked around the lake, among the children, dogs, bicycles, skates, pedal cars, carriages, pedal boats, no, no pedal boats, passing, in the iridescent dust, clusters of old men speaking Yiddish on the benches, who watched us go by.)

The Buttes-Chaumont where Albertine and Andrée sometimes went to walk and do things. . . . For, according to Andrée, "Albertine especially liked to do it in the countryside . . . when she didn't have the time to go far . . . we would go to a house in the Buttes-Chaumont she knew about or beneath the trees, where hardly anyone ever went."

Galliffet. It appears that du Lau and Haas later rebuffed him. There were rumors that he had appropriated his rank. In an article in *L'Intransigeant* in July 1902, Henri Rochefort made reference to this.

> Charles Haas, who passed away recently and whom I knew well, came to see me in London during my exile, after having spent two weeks with the Empress Eugénie in Farnborough. The widow of Louis Bonaparte had, at great length, told him about the visit that this same Galliffet had made to the ex-emperor, then a prisoner in Wilhelmshoehe. Galliffet had come to ask his former emperor to backdate a decree conferring the two stars. This would enable him to defend himself against the claim that he had appropriated his rank.

Haas's daughter cut out this article by Henri Rochefort and placed it in an album she began on her father's death on July 14, 1902. I looked through this album at the Paris home of Haas's great-granddaughter, Princesse Claude R———.

THERE IS A STORY about Haas. One day he found himself in the company of an English ambassador. For better or worse, he attempted to converse with the man about politics. The ambassador was looking attentively at Haas, which Haas of course found quite flattering. But after a few moments he realized that it wasn't his words that he was paying such close attention to. No, it was his left shoulder. Haas first thought that there was a stain on his suit. And he asked the Englishman about it. But it was nothing of the sort. What the ambassador had been examining so intently was a small gold pin on his vest to which his pince-nez was attached. He preferred that to a ribbon around his neck. "Now there's an idea," said the ambassador. "I'm going to introduce it in London." Charles Haas told this grand story, which naturally filled him with pride, to Gaston Jollivet. Jollivet repeated it in his *Souvenirs de la vie de plaisir sous le Second Empire* (1927).

An Exercise in Futility

PROUST CONTINUALLY TRIES TO CONVINCE US THAT SWANN never discusses serious subjects. To do so would be pedantic or pointless. Or both. Were the others, the Verdurins and Guermantes alike, too stupid to understand? You're the one who said it. No, Swann definitely preferred trivia, obviously specific kinds of trivia, with lots of detail, detail upon detail, all of it concrete. He was an expert on kitchen recipes and technical specifications. He charmed the men, drove the women crazy. "It was as if he put everything, money, intellect, everything, into the art of living so he would be pleasing to women. And naturally he received his due. Women were mad about him. But what distinction, what brilliance! And what a dandy! Ah, I can see him now, with his gray top hat lined with green." A description of Swann in the *Search?* No, Haas. But it's still Proust who is talking (to Céleste).

Was Swann condescending of others? Did he, monstrous egotist that he was, keep all that was richly serious for himself? Possibly. But in any event, he didn't take his own seriousness seriously. And during those inevitable moments when he did, when something serious, oh so inadvertently, through fatigue or some minor lapse, some self-betrayal, revealed him, he corrected his blunder with a swift return to irony. He's a dilettante. Swann lives, thinks, and speaks between quotation marks. It's likely that he was saving himself for another life. But which one? Everyone knows we have only one. One life. This gnaws at Proust, or rather the narrator, more than anything. It's difficult to realize the extent of his anguish. Yet, it's all quite fascinating. (The concessive is inappropriate here, for it's really a question of causality. In *Within a Budding Grove*, the narrator's mother is surprised that Monsieur de Norpois is "so precise although so occupied." Similarly, Proust adds, we shouldn't be surprised that the elderly are astonishing given their age, that kings are simple people at heart, and that country folk are knowledgeable about current events. We're not dreaming, he says, "for the 'althoughs' are really unrecognized 'becauses.'") So, it's not in spite of his dilettantism that Swann is fascinating, but because of it. This endless self-satisfaction of the dilettante, the life, so ostentatious, so insolent, given over to jealousy, a life of pure pleasure, of sensuality, a pure receptacle and only receptacle, without any hope of fecundation, is fascinating. A life of nothing, of little nothings, a meaningless life. Life. Proust was fascinated to see someone so in love with life and so obviously loved by her in return. Even if, when all was said and done, it was ruined. It's a great consolation to realize that, in the end, it was ruined. Now we have had our revenge, Proust, Marcel, and I.

Seated, for Days at a Time

I SPENT THE DAY SEATED IN THE MANUSCRIPT DEPARTMENT OF THE Bibliothèque Nationale. I had forgotten the story I had read that morning, the story of the dog with the big head, the child-pup, the grandmother, and Alain Delon. It wasn't until the evening, when I was in bed, that it came back to me. As well as the question of the relationship between that story and Haas. The answer was straightforward: there was none. Except, possibly, as I realized as I was falling asleep, that Delon played Charlus in a film by Volker Schlöndorff (1984) and that, at the B.N., it was Haas's letters to Comte Robert de Montesquiou that I had tried—quite unsuccessfully, since Haas's writing was so bad—to decipher.

It was strange, and no doubt coincidental, that Haas and Gilberte, a real person and a fictional character, had in common a particular way of writing. In the case of Gilberte, on at least two occasions Proust remarks that when she writes a *t*, the bar doesn't actually cross the letter but sits on top of it, as if she were underlining a word on the line above, and that the dots on her *i*'s interrupted the sentence above. But look at the way Haas writes the conjunction "and" (I'm transcribing the sign schematically): $\approx$.

ONE DECEMBER MORNING, I went to see Bernadette A———. We had spoken together before on the phone, twice I believe. You may recall that it was she who had initially thought my book was anecdotal. I now had the impression that all at once, or rather gradually, the subject began to fascinate her. I made use of her considerable expertise in "Proustology." Much greater than my own, of course. She pointed out several possibilities for further research—the memoirs of Boni de Castellane, the catalog of the Proust exhibition at the Jacquemart-André Museum (1971)—possibilities I had already researched. She was surprised. "But you know more than I do!" And why the hell shouldn't I know more than she? If she had known as much or more than me, she would have written this book herself. But, fearing that her comment was the expression of some genuine pain I may have caused her, I began apologizing, mumbling something or other to allay her fears.

Bernadette was about to leave for a Proust conference, where she would be speaking about Céleste in the countryside where she, Céleste, had grown up and where she, Bernadette, had just spent several days, in Lozère, among the sheep. . . . A painful realization struck me at that moment: what if she decided to. . . . And suddenly there was something, in her voice, her intonation, something . . . some suspicion.

She called me back. She wanted to invite me to a seminar. She was certain that Haas, that misunderstood character, would be of interest to the public. She sensed my hesitation. Maybe I didn't want to reveal my little project? Bernadette again began to disturb me. And what if she. . . ? She told me about a picture collection assembled by Georges Cattauï, which included, among other things, a portrait of Haas and his daughter, Luisita. I was later to see the original of this photograph at the home of Princesse Claude R——, Luisita's granddaughter. That same day I would also discover a letter from Charlotte D——, Luisita's daughter, to the writer Philippe Jullian. Charlotte had given Georges Cattauï some family photographs to give to Painter. Yet Painter, in the English edition of his Proust biography, stated, without further explanation, that Luisita's mother was Odette de Crécy, in other words, a whore! Charlotte's blood began to boil when she learned the news. She demanded that Painter change this unsubstantiated, and defamatory, claim in the French edition of his book. Which Painter did.

But there remained the question of my presence at the seminar. I was somewhat undecided. My work still seemed to me rather vague. My book wasn't beginning to crystallize. I didn't feel strongly one way or the other, and when I did, only intermittently. I was simultaneously burning with desire and afflicted by a kind of frigidity. Unless it was the fault of poor Haas, who certainly couldn't help it. But wasn't he just a shimmering phantom? Hadn't I become, like Swann, like the narrator, a being in pursuit of ephemeral figures, whose reality, solidity, or substance exists only in our imagination? Wasn't I, following their sorry example, just as likely to be taken for a sick man?

One day, a day of nonstop rain, I was overcome by a sudden frenzy of activity. I wrote a letter to the National Archives. I called the library at the Institut. I visited the archives of the prefecture of police. Nothing.

I spent the next few days sitting at tables in libraries or standing in front of file cabinets in the archives. Nothing. I looked at works about the Rothschild family without finding the least trace of any Antoine Haas, a high-ranking officer of the bank, skimmed the memoirs of countesses, viscountesses, and several duchesses. Nothing. At the Bibliothèque Nationale I found some frivolous material by Montesquiou. Some ideas about the Jews, the Affair, et cetera, in a letter to Joseph Reinach. But ideas aren't people. No more than dates. Or a genealogy.

In Le Monde, I read a complaint by a priest about Martin Scorsese's The Last Temptation of Christ, in which the author took issue with the reactions of the Catholic hierarchy. But the film was not a betrayal. For one good reason: the Gospels are silent about the psychology of Jesus. I continued to repeat the good priest's expression, "The Gospels are silent about the psychology of Christ," applying it to my own attempt to pinpoint Haas.

I said to myself that even if I had access to all the documents in the world and were able to reconstruct the essential aspects of his existence, this wouldn't tell me anything about anyone's inner life. No one's in fact. I had to acknowledge that I had no one. I thought I had tracked a hare, but, after a painful illness, he had long since gone to ground somewhere in the cemetery of Père-Lachaise. Was my instinct enough? A voice, a contrary voice, rose up in me, whispering the reassuring words that, perhaps, all things considered, the hare was indistinguishable from a swan. Regardless of what Proust has to say.

Haas *was* Swann. Of that, there is no doubt. Otherwise, how would his contemporaries, in 1913, have been able to so easily, so spontaneously identify him? Everything led me to believe that it was the swan that harbored the reality of the hare. *Hic jacet lepus.*

But I was insistent. I kept a daily record. I didn't even have Charles Haas's birth certificate. I didn't know if he was born in 1832 or 1833. Or even if he had been born, or where, or when. However, he was definitely dead. Even Proust says so. And *Le Figaro*, and *Le Gaulois*. . . . Yes, there is a mention in *La France juive* by the sinister Drumont. There is another in the catalog of a Proust exhibition, a Degas exhibition. In Proust's correspondence, edited by Philip Kolb, . . . and a reference. . . .

A phantom: "It was my fate to pursue only phantoms, beings whose reality existed for the most part in my imagination." At least I had the consolation, if not of getting closer to Haas, of getting a bit closer to Proust, and even to Swann, since they amounted to the same thing, since he had "filled" this "inner life"—what Proust called Swann's "humanity"—with the very inner life, the humanity that made him who he was, that is, Proust. Swann too "had a penchant for phantoms. Phantoms that were pursued, forgotten, pursued again, sometimes for no more than a single meeting, so he could touch an unreal existence that suddenly vanished." However, I could never imagine Haas as a troubled pursuer of ghosts. There were no phantoms for Haas.

That was the difference between the swan and the hare. Swann is inconceivable without Proust. More than a creation, he is an emanation of Proust. And yet, far into the *Search*, the narrator continuously tries to maintain the distance, everything that separates him from Swann: "even the most similar people, who, because their features are so comparable and the circumstances so similar, we choose to present as symmetric to one another, remain opposites in many respects."

I returned to the Bibliothèque de l'Arsenal. From there, I went to the archives of the city of Paris, quai Henri IV. I sat at seat number four, apparently reserved for civil court matters. I was waiting for them to bring me the records in which Charles Nathan Haas's name was most likely to appear. These were records for the military draft for the class of 1853 (section DR 1, nos. 70, 75, 76: fill out three different forms, then wait an hour next to a young man wearing a black skullcap, bent over an open notebook with the name Cahen on it, opposite a young woman who looked at me from time to time as if she recognized me or because I looked strange). Class of 1853 since I assumed Haas was born in 1833. But they only had the records for three arrondissements in Paris: the first, eighth, and tenth. The others had simply disappeared. Like looking for a needle. . . . After a while, while skimming through the names, I actually began to hope that I wouldn't find anything. Then I could leave here and light a cigarette. But I still didn't know what school young Charles Nathan had attended. (It is morning, and as I write these lines I still don't know. But I've lost any desire to find out.) I remember having read, at the beginning of *Swann in Love*, a passing reference to the fact that Swann had a friend with whom he had attended the École du Louvre. Now here was a possible source of information, and it was not at all improbable. For I had also learned that Haas had served as a fine arts inspector for three short years, between 1868 and 1871. He could easily have been to the school. I looked in the directory—there were two phone numbers. The first connected me with the choppy, mechanical voice of an answering machine. The second to the offices of the museum. I asked for the school (extension 3780). I asked my question. The woman referred me to the alumni association (extension 3677). That woman, a different woman, forwarded me to Ms. R——, librarian (extension 3124). Who just as quickly forwarded me to Monique L——, the author of an academic work on the school. So we spoke. I explained to her—I had first made a quick calculation—that my character would have attended the school around 1850 or 1860. Which was rather vague. On the other hand, it was fairly specific. For the fact of the matter is that the school didn't exist at that time. It wasn't created until 1882. Approximately at that time, Haas met a very beautiful woman with whom he would later have a daughter, and Swann, Odette. Obviously they were no longer youngsters. Aside from the fact that Haas could not have attended courses at the school, I came across this other bit of information: neither could Swann! Even by the standards of novelistic freedom inherent in the creative act, Proust's chronology was faulty. I promised myself that I would tell Bernadette A——. Wasn't this worth presenting a paper at the University of Alabama? The Institute for World Literature in Moscow? Shanghai? Zurich? Düsseldorf? Tokyo? Illiers? Cabourg?

A few days later, in spite of my discouragement, I telephoned the Institut de France at the Chantilly Museum. Yes, Haas's name appeared on the record. A young woman with a vulgar voice told me that it had something to do with the Duc d'Aumale. But because they were short staffed, she couldn't provide any additional information. I would have to go there in person. But not right away—they were repairing the heating system. And there were no stairs. Perhaps I could write? It didn't matter one way or the other since they were still short staffed. You couldn't do any research at the facility. I wondered what exactly it was that the woman on the phone was doing there? Other than telling people that they were short of personnel.

I took the risk of writing to the conservator. I soon received from the Institut de France's Condé Museum at the Château de Chantilly a photocopy sent by the conservator of the collections, Amélie L——, of a letter by Haas, dated, with considerable but incomplete precision, Sunday, October 14, of the then current year. I felt simultaneously satisfied and disappointed. I wanted to familiarize myself with his writing, which was nearly illegible. I grabbed my pen and began copying the letter, trying to decipher it as I went along. By imitating his writing, which looked like Arabic, perhaps I hoped for some magical effect that would have enabled me, through my appropriation, by allowing my pen to follow the trace of his own letters, which only very vaguely resembled the letters of the Latin alphabet, to uncover some secret, to discover where the hare was lurking. A waste of time, for my belief was indeed magical and superstitious.

Monsieur,

I hasten to accept the gracious invitation that Monseigneur the Duc d'Aumale has addressed to me for *Friday*, and request that you be kind enough to express to his Royal Highness my thanks and the respectful wishes of his devoted servant.

Very truly yours,
C. Haas

I was terrified; its triviality seemed to mock me.

I went to see Bernadette A—— one Thursday morning in December. She brought me stacks of books, placed them on the table, and had me sit down. Seated side by side, we searched. From time to time we exchanged a comment, or question. At one moment, unexpectedly, she asked me why I lived like this. I remained silent. She asked me again, Why had I decided to live like this? Her question was not so much indiscreet as enigmatic. Something told me that someone, probably recently, had also asked Bernadette the same question, using those very words, and under similar circumstances. Someone who, it seemed, secretly wanted to seduce her. Almost without realizing it, I answered that I hadn't chosen. The answer seemed to satisfy her and she returned again to her Proustian newsletters.

I came across a study devoted to Volker Schlöndorff's film. I read that Swann made love *a tergo* with a prostitute Odette may have known, or possibly had sodomized her. The news startled me. But no, he didn't sodomize her! According to Bernadette, the film was ambiguous. She leaned toward sodomy. The director had clearly wanted to draw Swann toward the character's English side. And of course it was well known that, in England, in the public schools, the teachers and older students sodomized the young. I didn't discuss this strange syllogism. Even so, I did acquiesce. However, something kept nagging at me: Swann didn't sodomize Chloé, the prostitute. Swann was somewhere else. As he is making love, he is standing, fully dressed, no less, and smoking. He was obsessed by Odette. Chloé didn't exist; she was there only to provide him with information. Nor was there any sense of gratification for Swann. There was no reason for Swann to sodomize her. This "amorous" disposition or, more precisely, this sexual configuration, would have been a sign of his desire for her, a sign that he sought in her a specific form of pleasure, a greater pleasure. That she filled him with desire. That she represented something for him, even if it were only his physical desire for her. Not even that. She represented nothing. And he was filled with anything but desire. He was driven by his insane anguish to find out if. . . .

I reread what Schlöndorff himself said about the actor he had chosen for the role (in an issue of the Proust Society newsletter):

> Jeremy Irons has that air of "British" elegance, the intellect and tact that were attributed to Charles Haas. Because of his handsome, melancholy features, his sensitivity, that sense of adolescence and narcissism, of being an eternal

outsider in the world, he allows us to see the author's interior world through him. His Swann links Haas and Proust together within a single fraternity.

There was no doubt about it: There was something English about Swann. Starting with his name. And there were other traits: his friendship, which he shared with Haas, with the Prince of Wales. And for Haas, the idea that England would be the final refuge for Jews if the intimidation caused by the Affair began to spread and deepen. This conversation seemed to interest Bernadette. She walked resolutely (her walk, her voice, her appearance were always resolute) to the phone and, on my behalf (or on her behalf?), asked a certain Suzanne V—— (of the V—— Bank), the daughter, if I understood correctly, of Baron Hottinguer, the owner of the Château de Guermantes near Lagny, in Seine-et-Marne, where she thought the Tissot painting from 1868, representing the balcony of the Cercle de la rue Royale, was located. She had never been there. She suggested that we go together for a private visit. . . .

Bernadette was divorced, the mother of an eleven-year-old daughter. At night she read Montesquieu and Voltaire to her. The language of the eighteenth century seemed to put the child to sleep. Recently she had switched to *Madame Bovary.* Yes, her daughter enjoyed it.

As I was in the hallway getting ready to leave, she suggested that we have lunch. I was evasive. I *had* to get back home, I said, as I studied her cherry red mouth, fleshy like a ripe summer fruit. Bernadette had her time to herself. She used to teach in a grammar school in one of the working-class suburbs. She had studied martial arts. She was incorrigibly talkative. I started thinking of Françoise Dolto—daughters are talkative because they don't have a penis. My own penis caused me to remain silent; I succeeded only in muttering a few words in between the rare moments of silence she allowed. Bernadette had the virtue of forcing me to say things to myself rather than out loud. And indeed, I told myself that if this young woman, who was obviously intelligent, gifted, and erudite, could really sit down to work instead of simply talking, she would write remarkable things. Had I been a Christian, I would have prayed for her. I felt sorry for Bernadette A——, a little like the narrator with respect to Swann. In fact, what is happening with Swann and his study of Vermeer? Unfortunately his work is still in the planning stage. Maybe it's just as well. For if, not content with being a man about whom it was said with admiration—or envy, the one not excluding the other—"He has everything going for him!" Swann had also decided to become a writer, it would have been intolerable. But there was nothing to fear. It was simply ontologically impossible. There was no reason to be jealous, to consider them rivals, "these irresolute and sterile amateurs." They are, according to Proust, "like those early machines that were unable to get off the ground but which contained, not the secret mechanism that had yet to be discovered, but the desire to fly." They are *poignant.*

BERNADETTE A—— CALLED me back. She had inquired about the Tissot painting. First, it had never been at the Château de Guermantes in Seine-et-Marne, but in Boissy-Saint-Léger, in some other property owned by that same Baron Hottinguer. The grandfather, who was given the painting after the men in the Cercle—whom it depicted—drew lots for it, had bequeathed it to his grandson, Henri. Consequently, the painting was now in Switzerland. (The Hottinguer Bank was connected with the V—— Bank, Swiss Protestants.) As a result I wouldn't be going to Guermantes with Bernadette. Or anywhere else for that matter.

On the telephone she frequently burst into laughter. Not only on the phone. She told me that that evening she was having dinner with I no longer remember which relative of Céleste Albaret. Her daughter? I had revealed to Bernadette that a friend who worked in television, Monique A——, had given me two original photographs of the entire Albaret-Gineste family. Monique A——— had saved these documents from a program on Proust, thinking they might interest me. She offered them to me as a present. I, in turn, wanted to offer them to Bernadette. But she immediately informed me that she intended to return them to their legitimate owner. And, depriving me of the pleasure of giving her, Bernadette, pleasure, she revealed her avarice, her anxiousness to get her hands on them. On the phone something told me that she wanted to come over and get them that very evening. I had, thank God, no need to lie to her: the photographs were in my office. That evening Bernadette A——— tired and annoyed me. The way she laughed at anything. Tissot, the Swiss, Suzanne V———, Hottinguer, Boissy-Saint-Léger—it was all a jumble. I no longer knew what was going on. Except for the vague feeling that I was right to feel disappointed. Switzerland! And winter sports, she said, laughing like a crystal chandelier that has been jostled. But that evening I was in no mood to laugh with her. And what about the pictures? She could stop by my office some morning. Yes, the morning. Silence. Wait. . . .

Haas in Love

When he was forty-eight or forty-nine years old, Haas had an affair with a Spanish noblewoman, the wife of the Marquis d'Audiffret. Her name was Adélaïde de Arellano. They had a daughter, Luisita, born in 1881. I looked at the chronologies for the *Search*, which some meticulous and learned scholars had so thoughtfully compiled. Any variation in the dates is so small as to be negligible. One of the chronologies claims that *Swann in Love* occurs between autumn 1880 and the beginning of the following year. Gilberte was born in 1881; Swann and Odette were wed in 1890.

According to another chronology, Swann first met Odette in 1879. Their relationship grew increasingly strained over the next year. Gilberte's birth is said to have taken place in October or November 1880 and her parents' marriage in 1889.

Not only did the chronologies agree to within a few months, and at most a year, but all the chronologies harmonized, although inadvertently, with Haas's love affair. Haas met Adélaïde in 1880; Luisita was born the following year. Haas and Adélaïde didn't marry, either because the woman was already married or, which is more likely, the idea of marriage had no appeal for Haas. Moreover, this woman was not a courtesan. There was nothing in common between her and Odette de Crécy, who had also once been married, but to a certain Comte de Crécy.

They do have something in common, however: the odor of scandal that, in both cases, clung to their relationships. Swann, a man of the world, marries a cocotte. Haas, a man of the world, has a child with a descendant of one of the oldest Spanish families, who also happened to be married to an extremely wealthy (and soon to be formerly wealthy) marquis from Nice.

BUT LET'S POSITION OURSELVES so we can get a better look at the surrounding landscape. Proust provides a strange analysis of the "Gallicized Jews." The antimodel is Bloch. About Bloch, Proust says that he wasn't ennobled through an alliance with England or Spain. He compares Bloch to the very noble Sir Rufus Israëls, whose wife, Lady Israëls, is none other than Swann's aunt. Swann doesn't like her, never really cultivated her, but is likely to be her heir. Sir and Lady Israëls have children, cousins of Swann, for whom he's a bit like a poor relation, rightly or wrongly. They call him "Cousin Bette," they think he's envious. One very Balzacian remark helps bring their attitude into focus: "Her husband's family, which was roughly on a par with the Rothschilds, had for several generations handled the business matters for the princes of Orléans."

For Bloch, Sir Rufus Israëls was practically royalty, "before whom Saint-Loup must have trembled." However, he was "in the Guermantes's circle a foreign parvenu, tolerated by them but a friend only of those who weren't concerned about their pride."

Speaking of Sir Rufus Israëls, Proust raises the subject of the power of "certain powerful Jews" before the Dreyfus affair. We learn, incidentally, that Swann, two years before his death, had become reconciled with his aunt. The intuition was pertinent. It was the Affair that caused the social fall of "certain powerful Jews" and also reconciled Swann, a convert and perhaps the child of a convert, with other Jews.

But I want to return to this bit of strangeness: Bloch was not ennobled by an alliance with England or Spain. And therefore he is not a "Gallicized Jew." It's hard to understand why such alliances with England or Spain were needed to be more French. This may be easier to understand if we return for a moment to the transition from Haas's name to Swann's. Haas's Gallicization occurs paradoxically through his English patronymic. The same phenomenon occurs in the transition from Jakob Rothschild to James. But Bloch, poor man, remains Bloch. Everyone is well aware that du Rozier is Bloch. And yet, for Lady and Sir Rufus, the noble titles *Sir* and *Lady*, which place them far above Bloch in the social hierarchy, do not in any way alter the fact that they are merely tolerated by the Guermantes.

This would all be quite contradictory if it were not for the Affair. For the Dreyfus affair suddenly revealed that there were no "Gallicized Jews." It was just a long-standing joke. There are only Jews. In one sense, from then on, the less a Jew wanted to be a Jew, the less Jewish he appeared, the less he behaved as Jews were supposed to behave, the less he adopted their rituals, their beliefs, or their social behavior, the more he became a Jew. That was the lesson learned from the Affair. A lesson that Jews failed to learn (except for a small, Zionist fringe). The others were, at best, content to be anticlerical and supporters of human rights. Much later, they thought Vichy was a misunderstanding. Nothing more than a misunderstanding. Some of them didn't hesitate to expose their strange cousins, the scabrous *Ostjuden*, to the discriminatory anti-Semitic laws. Yet the two branches of the same tree, the noble and the primitive, were severed by the same ax.

I'm getting carried away with myself.

Swann/Haas. Not Bloch. Swann has his English name. Haas has a quasi-conjugal affair with a woman who is of Spanish ancestry and a noble. Therefore, he is "ennobled," a "Gallicized Jew." What's more, since the woman, although an adulteress, is pious and even devoted, he converts. He does not say as did Madame Straus, "I have too little religion to change it." But the effect of the conversion, from a strictly social point of view, was nonexistent and almost resulted in ridicule. When Swann brings the Duchesse de Guermantes the proofs of his study of the coins minted by the Order of Saint-Jean of Rhodes, the duke has this to say: "It's unbelievable, this mania people have to study other people's religion." Yet it's Swann that's being discussed here. Precisely. Swann converted, although when or why is unclear. It had zero social effect. Swann suffers from the fact that all the Guermantes are anti-Semites—and says as much. Why then does he insist on seeing them, even when he's at death's door? Then there's Haas and the Jockey Club. He was a member up to the end, in spite of his support for Dreyfus. And he sided with the Jockey Club, along with du Lau, against Galliffet, a republican, a Dreyfusard, and a military reformer. Contradiction? The Affair created a fault line in French society, of that there is little doubt, but it also did so within the Jewish community and within each Jew as well. That's because when one is a "Gallicized Jew" (the expression is Proust's), the fault is already there, between being a Jew and being French. The fault can simply deepen. The Affair provided the "right opportunity," as Haas says to Joseph Reinach concerning the rumor spread by the teeming horde of the self-righteous: "there are too many Jewish officers in the French army."

A FINAL WORD about the mating game among Proust's characters, which he describes as follows:

> Like those interspecies crossbreeding experiments practiced by Mendelians or found in mythology, Swann, as an artist, was thought to have experienced a certain pleasure in mating with a being of a different race, an archduchess or a cocotte, in contracting a royal alliance or marrying below his station.

What is seductive in the above quotation is that the real and the fictional are symmetrically distributed along divergent but, from the aesthetic point of view shared by Proust and Swann, equally interesting paths. Swann, as we know, married a courtesan. However, we do not know if Proust knew that Haas had an affair (with scandalous results) with a woman of the high Spanish nobility, a descendant of the royal dynasty of Trastámara—Pedro the Cruel, king of Castille and León; Isabel the Catholic; Juana the Mad (*la Loca*), whose mother was a distant relative of the Empress Eugénie.

For Proust, ennoblement via England or Spain would be a means for a Jew to become truly French. At best it's a bizarre claim. And yet. . . .

Adélaïde, Haas's paramour, is Spanish to the bone. With respect to this alliance between England and Spain, I found the following curiosity in a dictionary. An ancestor of Adélaïde, Henry of Trastámara, known as Henry the Magnificent, brother of Pedro the Cruel, appealed to Bertrand du Guesclin in his struggle to overthrow his brother, who was supported by Edward, Prince of Wales, the Black Prince, and Pedro. . . .

Of course Odette is neither English nor Spanish. Yet, in the overall economy and genesis of the *Search*, her character is interwoven with fine strands of English and Spanish thread. Proustologists know that in the various "sketches" that constitute Proust's *Notebooks*, Odette is not yet Odette, but *Carmen* (just as Swann, in this prehistory of the *Search*, represents Proust himself, before he splits into Marcel and Charles Swann). Was it under the influence of the obsolete *cocodette* (a word that had entered the French language around 1870) that Carmen became Odette? Odette has even less to do with the English. However: (1) In Nice, where she had once lived, "it is said that, still a child, she was handed over by her mother to a rich Englishman." (2) From her former husband, the Comte de Crécy, Pierre de Verjus, who goes by the Anglo-Saxon patronymic Saylor, we learn that the family (whose motto, playing on the family name, is *"Ne sçay l'heure"*) is an "authentic branch, detached in France, of the English family that bears the Crécy title." It is unknown whether Saylor, a very wealthy man who was discreetly despoiled by Odette, was that same very rich Englishman to whom, "still a child," her mother had handed her. It doesn't look that way. But so what. (3) Odette's linguistic tics. There seems to be no end to this Frenchwoman's anglicisms, the affected lexicon of her franglais. She doesn't *fish for compliments*. She has a *home*. She finds certain neighborhoods quite *smart*. Refers to a gathering of socialites as a little *meeting*. Celebrates *Christmas* by preparing *pudding*. She says, rather technically, *patronizing*; refers to the young narrator as a *gentleman* and invites him for a *cup of tea*. She clamps her teeth together to give the expression a "slightly British" accent. She says she is going *to meet* someone. Asks about their *babys* [*sic*]. Of course she says *good-bye, good evening*, and *good morning*. Sacrifices to *five o'clock tea*. Serves *toasts*. Has her husband order visiting cards where *Mr.* appears before the name Charles Swann. She arranges it so that Bergotte now writes the *lead article* in *Le Figaro:* "He will be exactly *the right man in the right place*." Compliments Marcel on his *nurse*: "I didn't know English but soon realized that the word referred to Françoise." She neologizes at the drop of a hat: she's delighted that you didn't *drop* her completely. And so on. In short, the woman is an Anglomaniac.

Finally, do we know when Swann and Odette were united, when they "adjusted the orchid" for the first time? This information would allow us to connect the date with an event in real time: it turned out to be the day of the festival of Paris-Murcia, which was held to assist victims of the flooding in Murcia, Spain.

Between the *Search* and reality there is a remarkable chiastic union, in which "royal alliance" is coupled with Spain and "cocotte" with England.

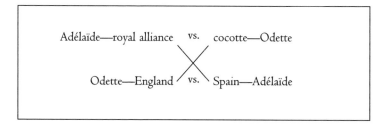

Adélaïde—royal alliance   vs.   cocotte—Odette

Odette—England   vs.   Spain—Adélaïde

According to Proust, this represented the sense of pleasure, at least for Swann the "artist," to be found in exotic couplings, the kind of crossbreeding practiced by "Mendelians," the voluptuous aesthetics of advantageous or—and why not?—disadvantageous alliances.

LUISITA PASSED AWAY in 1956. She left behind a daughter, Charlotte, who married one Franck Delmas, and a granddaughter, Claude, who would become Princesse Mario R——. There were two R——'s in the telephone directory: rue de Varenne and rue de l'Université.

Luisita and her husband, Noël Perret, had lived in Algeria. Sometime around 1930, the couple decided to return to Paris. They stored their furniture in a warehouse, which was destroyed by a fire. Everything Luisita had inherited from her father was gone: furniture, paintings, curios. Only a handful of letters and a few photographs, which were already in France, were spared. I had to find this Princesse Mario R——, rue de Varenne, rue de l'Université, or wherever she might be. To do this I had to identify Prince Mario R——, whose wife—in actuality, his second wife—was the great-granddaughter of Charles Haas. Eventually I found him, but it wasn't easy.

The princess lived sometimes on quai d'Anjou in Paris and sometimes in M——, in the south. I was struck by the coincidence: Swann lived in an old townhouse on the quai d'Orléans, a neighborhood, according to Odette, "that was not at all smart for a man like Swann, who was himself so smart." A judgment that was shared by the narrator's grandmother. For my part, I know of several people that would be more than happy with his old house on the quai d'Orléans. Only a short step separated the real quai d'Anjou of the real great-granddaughter from the fictional quai d'Orléans of the fictional great-granddaughter. What pleasure in mating, in crossing categories that would normally remain distinct. But what did "normally" mean?

Haas's great-granddaughter! At home that's all I could talk about.

I wrote to her and anxiously awaited her response. I told myself that I was the first one to contact the family since . . . 1890. I prepared genealogies for Charles, gradually substituting for the unknowns the names I discovered, as if, like an explorer of remote islands, I were drawing a map, always pushing farther into the blank spaces of its terrae incognitae. I dreamed of La Pérouse. The name was very familiar to Swann, who knew all there was to know about "this explorer whose remains were brought back by Dumont d'Urville." He confided to General de Froberville, "La Pérouse was a wonderful character and I'm very interested in him." Of course, La Pérouse, as everyone knows, is the name of the street where Odette lived. In making these apparently aberrational juxtapositions, producing monsters, just like the Mendelians, I feared losing the way, like La Pérouse himself, in some dangerous territory, where I might disappear body and soul, killed by a vindictive arrow.

Each morning I waited for the mail to arrive, hoping to find a letter from boulevard Courteline in M———. The wait was likely to be long. There was no sign from the princess, and I didn't dare call.

One day, however, I swore I would call the *very next day*. And this was that next day.

"Monsieur Haas?" a man's voice asked. I found the mistake comical.

"No, this is. . . . But I was in fact calling about Charles Haas."
"One moment."

That morning I had tried twice to call the princess. The woman I had assumed was the maid—she had a heavy Spanish accent—told me that "Madame" took her lunch at one o'clock and that she was still at the "chalet."

I finally reached the princess at 1:10. She immediately asked me how I had managed to obtain her address. I greatly enjoyed detailing the various steps I had taken to find her. She had very few artifacts—a few letters, some photographs. Not long ago, however, a close friend had considered doing a book on Haas but finally gave it up because he couldn't find enough material. Proust had based Swann's character partly on Haas. Partly, she insisted. . . . He was a dandy, nothing more. . . . There wasn't much to say about him.

Oh, how I enjoyed hearing those words, no matter how discouraging. Or, curiously, because they were discouraging. The princess's voice, her tone sounded deliciously *simple.* But was there any reason for a princess not to be simple? According to Proust, wasn't the authenticity of the true princes measured precisely by their simplicity?

She had come up to Paris to supervise some work in her apartment. She was certainly willing to meet me but feared only that I would be disappointed. I, I had no such fears. To see her, hear her, was all I wanted, all I dreamed of. It was as if I were about to touch, yes, physically touch, what I can only describe as the *reality of the* Search, *the reality of the words of the* Search, *the reality of the imaginary world that appears in the* Search, *the reality of its objects of desire.* However, my intention was not as barbaric as it may seem. For it was not my intention to destroy more than the imaginary dimension of this work: its character as a work of art, its necessarily imaginary status, since it was a work of art. No, I wanted to verify that in fact I still understood it poorly (and am still not convinced that I understand it any better). To verify. To grope blindly somewhere behind the work, along its corridors, its foundations, its unexplored basement, its *depth* (although I was not unaware of the fact that a novel lacks depth since it is only made of words), the geological strata, themselves imaginary, that I thought, no doubt naively, gave it support. But my search was harmless. I would destroy nothing, cause no harm. I was no barbarian, because what I was looking for, the unnamed, the unidentifiable object, a kind of UVO, or unidentified virtual object, that had arrived here one day and contacted me, was itself imaginary. Just like the Duchesse de Guermantes, the pretext for so many daydreams, and the name Guermantes with which she is associated, or Odette for Swann, or Venice, or to see Berma in *Phèdre*, or whatever.

The princess soon arrived in Paris. She was moving from the third floor of the building on the quai d'Anjou to the second or fourth, that's all I knew. It was the reason she had "come up" to Paris. However, it was going to take time for her to locate the few cartons of documents from her mother and grandmother. She had been in Paris for two weeks and would remain there another three before returning to M———. Belatedly, I grew angry with myself for not saying to her that just to meet her, with or without any documents, would have pleased me. That I would have liked to speak with her or, rather, listen to her speak to me; would have liked her to transmit something of the family legend, stories about Haas, or what her mother, Charlotte, had said about him or, better still, her grandmother, *Swann's daughter!* I was becoming Marcel. I said to myself, using his own words: that name—Haas—has become almost mythological for me. I was pining away, waiting to hear her say it. But then I asked myself, with what imaginary object of desire by the name of Gilberte was I in love? I still don't know.

Gilberte Swann. Luisita Haas. How could I decide which of those names was more fictional than the other?

CHARLOTTE, LUISITA'S DAUGHTER, was born in 1903, that is, one year after Haas's death. She wrote a short memoir—no more than a few pages long—about her grandparents, Charles and Adélaïde. Adélaïde Rendon y Cabrera's family lived in Madrid, in a mansion that contained its own chapel. It was a noble family and fairly well to do. Her father, Víctor Rendon, a diplomat and writer, died in 1859.

When she was fifteen, Adélaïde, still a young girl, although extremely beautiful, was walking one day with her governess on the shore of Lake Retiro in Madrid, when she crossed the path of a middle-aged man—he was thirty-six—who seemed very old to her. This was the Marquis Léon-Barthélemy d'Audiffret. He followed her. The marquis was shocked, however, when he saw her enter the home of friends of his in the city. He decided to pay them a visit at once and in their presence declared his admiration for the lovely young daughter of the house. His friends, happy to see him again, did not refuse him when he returned the following day to ask for the child's hand in marriage.

The Marquis d'Audiffret was immensely wealthy. He owned a princely estate, surrounded by grounds that, after being divided up, would later become one of the city's most aristocratic quarters. One of its streets still bears the name of his wife: rue Adélaïde.

That city is Nice.

Odette de Crécy. Adélaïde Rendon y Cabrera. It's hard to see any connection between them. But consider the following: (1) Odette lived in Nice. (2) She was "handed over, still practically a child, to a rich Englishman." (3) Adélaïde was handed over, still practically a child, to a rich aristocrat . . . from Nice.

For Adélaïde the whole affair must have resembled a romantic fairy tale. For her marriage, celebrated in Madrid, she received an immense doll decorated with costly jewels.

The couple settled in Nice on the Marquis d'Audiffret's estate. Three daughters were born to them: Marguerite, Dolorès, and Marie-Thérèse. They were sent to a convent in Paris. Little by little, the marquis began to dissipate his fortune. He made a number of conquests, whom he forced his wife to receive in their home. Adélaïde grew morose, although she was very close with the Prince of Monaco and the wife of the Emperor Maximilian.

Then Adélaïde went up to Paris. There she soon entered the ranks of the aristocracy of the Second Empire. She later became a friend of Madame de Poilly and was often seen at her salon on rue du Colisée. Its habitués included: Barbey d'Aurevilly, François Coppée, Paul Bourget, Arsène Houssaye, Edmond de Polignac, Galliffet, Montesquiou, . . . and Charles Haas.

When she was seventeen, Annette du Hallays-Coëtquen had married the Comte de Brigode and, after his death, the Baron de

Poilly. She had an estate at Folembray, in Aisne, where she had a raised stage installed in the park. They performed works by Sedaine, Marivaux, and Maupassant.

It was in this salon, around 1880, that Charles and Adélaïde first met and grew close to one another. Nine months later a daughter was born. The birth took place in Spain and was surrounded by the greatest secrecy.

It had been a long time since the Marquis and Marquise d'Audiffret had lived together. But divorce was out of the question. The child's birth was obviously going to cause a scandal. A cousin of Adélaïde, who was no less than the governor of Toledo, came to her assistance. He provided the child with the necessary papers. He would be the godfather and Adélaïde the godmother.

Jesusa Maria Josefa Luisa Ramirez de Arellano, "mother and father unknown," was born August 25, 1881, at 9 Carretera de Aragon (Madrid), and was entered into the baptismal records of the parish church of San José de Madrid on September 17, 1881.

What was to be done with this child?

There is an unfinished letter from Madame d'Audiffret to Charles Haas, whose existence I learned of from the princess. It was written about 1884.

> I have just received a letter from Annette [Madame de Poilly] in which this *excellent friend* informs me that you have disappeared from Paris and that you are undoubtedly busy forgetting me . . . and that it's indeed my fault, that I *ought* to remain in Paris, etc., etc., etc. Ah, yes, another old fool that I'm not unhappy about keeping my distance from. . . . That Luisita is truly a prodigy. She already knows French a little and even by sight understands everything. I talk to her about Amélie so she can get used to her, but for the sake of her sanity I would like to know *who she intends to be for her.* I thought I heard you say that she would present her as *her niece.* We must tell Luisita *right now* what is *always* going to be said because she told Malvina and me that "she doesn't want to be deceived!!!!"

Imagine, she is so aware that she calls me Madrina out loud and whispers it in my ear. She gives me an endearing look and calls me "my little *maman*," something no one told her to say. For her age she's really marvelous, especially since she understands the *nuances* of things that are otherwise so mysterious. If Amélie is planning to *adopt her*, it's better to tell her right away that she is going to live with her *real mother*. Tell me quickly what you think of this, Charles, for with a little girl like her, you have to pay attention to all the details. You should also know that you can reason with her and that she obeys *as if she were eighteen years old*. She has an amazing mental capacity, so that if Amélie intends to be only her aunt, I must tell her, since she never stops asking me about it! I really wish that everything you've promised comes true, but once burned!! . . . We are justified in complaining when we suffer, just as Christ wept in the garden of olive trees and . . .

Tell me if it's possible for Amélie to make her her heir without bringing her up? . . . I assure you I don't have much, which you know, but it hurts me so much to leave her that money matters little and, as long as I have four sous in my pocket, I'll do what I can for her, I'll give her everything she needs, but *unfortunately* the future looks *bleak,* however, with your support and considering what Amélie would do for you, won't her future be assured? . . . Try to put yourself in my place and you'll understand everything, but I'm warning you that my sacrifice . . .

We'll go to the photographer. You can't imagine what a beauty she is. . . . Luisa's eyes and hair are superb . . . she looks sad, *concerned,* but she is happy, lively, and you'd die laughing to see her dance the *jota* and the fandango . . . and her character?? *horrible.* I have no idea how we're going to calm her down—this is the biggest calamity of her life; we're putting together toys and pretty clothing for the event because Luisa is *crazy* about being *chic* and elegant, her greatest worry, her most violent anger will melt away when she's presented with a pretty pair of bronze-colored shoes or a new dress! . . .

Yesterday, she asked me: "So, who do I belong to?" "You're *mine*," I told her, while kissing her, "*mine*, and your handsome papa's." Then she said, "And what about Mamamélie who waits on me, she's a mother like Malvina, a mother who isn't a *godmother*? I don't want to have a real mother except you, my godmother-mother. . . ."

Try to get here as soon as possible, Charles, so that together we can put these torments and problems to rest. I can't tell you how happy I am at the thought of seeing you again.

A letter from Haas to Adélaïde (whom he called "Mamita"). It's dated July 1885. Luisa is four years old.

My dear Mamita, my thoughts are always with you during this trip and I'll never forget that sad, sweet departure; I felt your heart beat for me, and poor little Luisa was determined to give me big kisses and show me just how much she loved me for as long as she could. I wonder what goes on in that funny and charming little head of hers? . . . Am I to understand that when she left, I was the only one who didn't displease her and that she no longer needs to worry about who I am until she is with me again? The poor child is not even able to use the little phrase she learned, "Hello, my little papa." What a dear child, so sweet, so spiritual, so gentle. Whenever I've seen her cry it's been only from sadness, never spite, never capriciousness. And now she has left for the "aguas."

Proust: "She [Gilberte] had even added, demeaning herself to raise herself up, 'Many things have been said about my birth, but I must ignore them all.'" And Proust continues, "Naturally, Gilberte didn't always go as far as when she insinuated that she was the daughter of some great individual."

Gilberte enjoyed surrounding her birth with an air of mystery. The belated shame she felt about her father is no less mysterious. She preferred to invent a "family romance." This mystery, which she complacently allowed to hover around her origins, is both a false mystery (Gilberte is consciously the instigator) and a fictional mystery.

However, a real mystery surrounded the birth of Luisita, whose godmother, Adélaïde, was in fact her mother. She was made to believe, for at least a time, that a woman named Malvina was her mother. Then, that Amélie was her real mother, but she should call her her aunt. In the midst of all this obfuscation and confusion, she was told that she could call this mysterious Monsieur Charles her "little papa." As if he weren't. What one admires most in this child is not her elegance, her wit, her gentleness, or the fact that she could dance the *jota* or the fandango. It was her sanity.

Gilberte: "I feel so good when I'm around my little papa. . . ." And Swann answers her: " 'You're a good daughter,' in a tone of voice softened by the sense of uncertainty about the future that is inspired in us by our excessive tenderness toward a being destined to outlive us."

Charles Haas to Luisa:

> My dear little Sita, do you believe that this morning my robe caught fire? Although I wasn't hurt, the robe is full of holes. Fortunately the smoke from the flames warned me of the accident. However, I immediately thought about my dear child. . . . Please be careful, my love; you know that I could go up in smoke in a moment's time. . . . I'm about to leave for Dijon and tomorrow evening I'll most likely be in Paris. . . . Perhaps I'll find a little letter from you. . . . Don't be lazy with your father my dear child, that would hurt me a great deal. . . . Give a big kiss to your aunt for me.

In May 1890 Haas openly acknowledged Luisita as his daughter. From then on she was to use his name. She wrote to him from the Convent of the Assumption in Lourdes, calling him succes-sively "My Dear Monsieur Haas"—signing her letters "Your Little Friend"—then "My Dear Papa," and later on "My Dear Father." Her letters were very devout. "I pray for you every day, especially since receiving your letter where you told me that this made you happy." Haas asked her to write to his friends, Mon-sieur de Saint-Joseph and Madame de Poilly at Folembray. And to send them (holy) "pictures." "If I speak to you of these little prayers, it's because you'll find consolation in them for your lit-tle sorrows, which are caused by your nervousness. . . . Yes, I al-ways have a headache."

It was most likely Adélaïde's influence that led Haas to con-vert to Catholicism. Luisita asked him if he still wore the medal she had sent him. "I hope so."

The Marquis d'Audiffret died at the hospital of the Broth-ers of Saint-Jean-de-Dieu. The marquise took the veil with the Society of Marie Réparatrice in Toulouse, in March 1892. (To punish herself? More likely because Haas never wanted to marry her and she now realized that he would become the child's legal guardian.) Luisita was getting ready to make her first communion. She stayed at the convent until she was eigh-teen. Her studies were interspersed with travel and vacations in Italy, all of which were gifts from her father.

Speaking of a medal, Proust wrote:

> These affectations contrasted with the sincerity of her prayers, especially those to Our Lady of Laghet, who had, when she was living in Nice, cured her of a mortal illness. Because of this she always wore a gold medal of Our Lady to which she attributed unlimited powers.

Like Swann, but for very different reasons, I struggled for a long time with Odette's past. First, because Adélaïde and her Marquis d'Audiffret had stayed in Nice. I was certainly not try-ing to establish the fact that Adélaïde *was* Odette. That would have been absurd. There was even a good chance that Proust had never heard of her. Charles and Adélaïde had never lived together. What's more, in 1892, she entered the convent where she would—or so it seems—end her days following the death of her husband, from whom she had been separated for years, thus expiating, I suppose, her extraordinary sins. Or simply because she realized that Charles didn't want to take care of her.

My real pleasure lay in identifying the thread of fortuitous complicity between Proustian fiction and reality, which I suddenly succeeded in revealing, just as Swann had, and with the same sense of "idolatry," the same aesthetic mania, in looking for equivalents between works of art and the faces of the real people he encountered. In doing so I did not feel I was degrading art to the trivial status of a reality meant only to be reproduced. This was certainly not the case. For I felt I could swell the work past its borders, adding to the turbulence of its floodwaters, helping it overrun and inundate the limitless field beyond. Perhaps I wanted to pursue the work of art, the way we pursue an object that flees before us, but perhaps also in the sense that I simply, yet irrationally, wanted to prolong its existence. And maybe, through this torrent of abundance I had imposed upon the work, I was hoping that it would touch everything around it, everything, including me. Until then I had been content to watch in safety from the shore. But what was intolerable in the work of art was precisely its disdainful sense of closure, the fact that it rejected us, held us painfully at arm's length, turning us into a bunch of unruly children, admonishing us to look at but not touch the coveted object. Thus, in retrospect my small undertaking had all the characteristics of a transgression that condemned me before I had even begun.

For that reason I had to try to clarify what it was about Our Lady of Laghet and the medal on which Swann made Odette swear that she had never had relations with women, knowing it represented a nearly magical object of veneration for her. I wrote to the shrine, which turned out to be not in Nice but in La Trinité, which was not far from there. Sister Marie Véronique graciously sent me two issues of the *Messager de Notre-Dame de Laghet*, three postcards of the sanctuary and the miraculous virgin, . . . and the medal. Especially the medal. Looking at Odette's medal, it was now my turn to be in the grip of some magical power, to be an "idolater," like Swann or, better yet, like Ruskin, whom Proust reproached for considering an architectural form to be beautiful, although the only beauty it contained was the symbol it embodied. I held in my fingers an object that Odette herself had touched. A holy relic. . . .

In her letter, Sister Marie Véronique asked me if Proust had known Our Lady of Laghet and under what circumstances. I had no idea. She also asked me for a short article on the subject for an issue of the *Messager*. "I would also be interested," she added, "in a photocopy of the passage in the book where the medal is discussed."

I must admit that I was somewhat put out by the sister's request. For one thing, I had no idea where Proust had learned of the shrine or the medal with the effigy of the miracle-working Madonna. Perhaps during a trip to Nice, while visiting the area? But maybe he never visited the shrine and had been satisfied to question someone who had worn the medal. Moreover, in the *Search*, the medal is referred to during a scene in which Swann makes Odette swear that she has never done "it" with women. Could I say that to Sister Marie Véronique? Wouldn't she be offended? I decided to tell her and transcribed the passages in question for her. And that's where things stood. . . .

From time to time I would look at the medal in its plastic sleeve. On the front appeared the Virgin and child; on the back, the sanctuary of Laghet. I thought about Odette, about Proust, about the Marquise d'Audiffret, Adélaïde, my two Charles's, and gentle little Luisita, so happy, yet so sad, suggesting to her "dear little papa" that he continue to wear the medal she had given him. How I would have liked to see and touch the real medal, compare it with the *actual fictional medal* of Laghet, the one worn by Odette, . . . which I had in front of me, as I examined it with a magnifying glass, as if I were trying to discover some secret inscription, an impossible sign intended for me and me alone.

I imagined an entire constellation of figures, who stood neither on the shore of fiction nor on that of reality, but somewhere else, somewhere within a dream. Which was, of course, none other than the slightly baroque dream . . . of my book.

Combray—Illiers—Folembray

Proust: "Swann's former girlfriends paid a great deal of attention to Gilberte."

Charlotte, Luisa's daughter, writes in her short memoir: "Charles Haas's friends doted lovingly on the little girl it gave him such pleasure to introduce. They took turns spoiling her, playing host, taking her on trips during the vacations allowed her by the convent where she was living."

Luisita: "My dear father. I received some charming letters from Madame de Poilly, Madame de Saint-Joseph, Madame Holande [*sic*], Madame Bourée (?). Violette hasn't answered me, but I hope she received my picture as well as the Princess (*Princesse Mathilde? Princesse d'Essling?*)."

I noticed that Proust speaks of Swann's former girlfriends, while Charlotte, referring to Haas, speaks of his male friends. And what about Luisita? Her letter refers exclusively to women; of the six names mentioned, all six are women. The conclusion? Proust is right. The novel is more credible than the real: Proust has managed to rectify what reality sometimes distorts.

Luisita often spent summers at Folembray, with the Baronne de Poilly. Her father would join her there and together they would go to the "*aguas*" at Challes-les-Eaux in Savoy. While reading Élisabeth de Gramont, I learned that Annette de Poilly had a bungalow built in the Pré-Catalan, in the Bois de Boulogne, known as "Les Ramiers," where she spent her afternoons during spring. In *Swann's Way* wasn't the Pré-Catalan—owned by Jules Amiot, the husband of "Aunt Léonie"—the place in Illiers that abuts the steep path through the hawthorns that one had to take to get to Swann's house in Tansonville?

Proust scholars know that Combray, until 1913, was none other than Illiers, and that, after 1914, Proust decided to integrate the war into his book. In his omnipotence he shifted Combray from the Eure to the Aisne.

Tuesday, July 6, Folembray, Aisne

My Dear Father,

I just received your kind letter, which made me very happy. I can't wait for your arrival since I'm very bored. Madame de Poilly will most likely return tomorrow. When you leave, I must remind you to bring some warm clothing because it's very cold here. The yellow boots with thick soles will be fine; you can easily find them at the Louvre. Along with my alpaca skirt, I would like my blue jacket. . . .

In the morning I get up at 8:30. I go to the park until lunch, then, later on, Madame Ollivier and I go for a long walk. Yesterday I gathered an enormous bouquet of wild flowers that I put in a vase in the salon. Then we come back for a snack. I drink a big glass of milk and then I water the flowers. I read in the park until dinner and in the evening I go to bed at 9:30. That's what I do at Folembray. I hope we'll soon be leaving for Challes.

I learn, again in Élisabeth de Gramont's memoirs, that Folembray was the center of German operations during the war. The château served as von Kluck's headquarters. In 1917 the Germans gratuitously destroyed the building, "even destroying the cemetery where the baroness's remains lay." She had died in 1905.

Folembray and Combray number 2 were located some fifteen kilometers from Laon:

I knew that Mademoiselle Swann often went to Laon for a few days; even though it was several kilometers away, this distance was made shorter by the fact that there were few obstacles, et cetera.

In September 1914 Gilberte wrote to the narrator that, fearing the German bombardments of Paris, she had, *as a last resort*, decided to take the train to Combray, precisely where the Germans had invaded following the French defeat at La Fère. Gilberte herself was forced to house the German general staff.

Love, Now and Forever . . .

In 1869 Sarah Bernhardt played in François Coppée's *Le Passant* to wide acclaim. She presented the play, among others, at the home of the Baronne de Poilly, to whom Coppée offered the manuscript. It is most likely in 1869 that Haas received the following note from Arthur Meyer (which I read at the home of the Princesse R—— on the quai d'Anjou):

> Dear Sir and Friend,
>
> An attractive woman, intelligent and artistic, wants me to bring you to see her—you lucky Don Juan! When do you want me to satisfy this desire?

Haas was thirty-seven, Sarah twenty-five. Reading the letters from Sarah to Charles, letters from a woman who is clearly in love, passionate, and filled with longing, Haas doesn't seem to be especially taken with her. Other indicators, however, lead me to believe that Haas in love must have been a kind of anti-Swann, or anti-Proust. In fact, it is clear that Swann was much closer to Proust than he was to Haas: "I began to take an interest in her character because of the similarities with my own." Proust wasn't lying then when he claimed that he had "filled" Haas with a very different sort of humanity. For it seems that what ultimately characterized Haas was his frivolity—at least on a psychological level, which included the ability to love. As for the rest, the social and worldly aspect of the man, he was completely the opposite: he shared his extreme sophistication with Swann, an aspect of his character that Proust, in spite of all his efforts, would never succeed in equaling. Proust had to find some other way to draw attention to himself—like writing books.

From Sarah Bernhardt to Haas (1869):

> Happiness has turned its back on me. I've suffered a great deal; I suffer a great deal; and in spite of my occasionally childish love, my heart is that of a woman, and that heart beats for you. This all sounds very dramatic to someone as frivolous as you. Maybe you laugh too much! All the better! As for me, I cry a great deal!
>
> I have a pain in my chest and I owe much of my suffering to you. My lips are continually dampened by this bloody froth. Could it be the kiss of death? Good-bye, my dear Charles. I feel for you an indefinable tenderness. I adore you; you do not love me; you cannot change that!
>
> Nor can I.
>
> I blow you a kiss filled with love.

Bernhardt's wonderful tirade would have done credit to Dumas *fils*. Yet even in Swann we find something like this same sense of frivolity, which seems to be typical of Haas. This comes through most clearly in the often quoted last sentence of *Swann in Love*, "To think that I've wasted so many years." And here Proust writes that Swann also displayed "that intermittent boorishness that reappeared in him whenever he was no longer unhappy."

I do not believe that Haas, when in love, was truly, or frequently, unhappy. My conclusion hangs on a slender thread: he didn't have it in him. What Proust refers to, speaking of Swann's "boorishness," is nothing more than his self-control. "You always manage to remain calm," Odette says to him at the beginning of their affair, "I don't know what it is about you." Sarah could have said the same thing about Charles Haas. She comes quite close, "This all sounds very dramatic to someone as frivolous as you." Elsewhere, she writes, "And you, my poor friend, whom I've snatched from his cherished idleness and thrust into my life. . . . Charles, I love you. Why? Oh, damned if I know, but that's the way it is. Don't laugh, I can see you from here."

An idle being, frivolous and calm, who laughs at the passion another feels for him. A swan, in other words.

Death Has Overtaken . . .

ONE EVENING IN 1901, HE HAD GONE TO DINE WITH THE PRINCESSE
d'Essling. Luisita was not feeling well, and he returned early to
85 avenue de Villiers. He went up to his daughter's room to see
how she was and tell her about his evening. She had been living
with her father ever since leaving the convent, two years earlier.
Around two o'clock in the morning, the girl was awakened by a
loud noise coming from the living room that separated her bed-
room from her father's. She ran to his room, where she found
him on the floor, his right hand gripping the cloth from a table
he had overturned during his fall. Terrified, too weak to lift him,
she called the valet. They sent for Charles's doctor, who didn't
arrive until four in the morning. He diagnosed it as a stroke. For
weeks Haas hovered between life and death. One side of his face
was paralyzed, making it difficult to understand what he was
saying. His hair had turned white, his profile had altered and
now assumed a distinct curvature. There had been no damage to
the brain and the paralysis gradually disappeared. Haas began to
resume his normal life, although at a somewhat slower pace. He
made few visits himself, but in the afternoon there were many
guests: the Marquis du Lau, the Princesse d'Essling, the
Comtesse de Froissia-Broissia, the Ganays, the Comtesse Ad-
heaume de Chevigné-Modène. . . .

During the winter of 1901 to 1902, on his doctor's recommendation, the Princesse d'Essling encouraged Haas to rent a villa in Nice, opposite her own. They made daily excursions in her carriage and received visitors, including the Prince d'Essling and the Duc de Mouchy.

In April Haas returned to Paris, where he resumed his life as before. He spent time at his club. One day in spring, he was invited to lunch at Cavé's villa in the Bois de Boulogne, which adjoined that of Madame Howland. As he was getting into the carriage, Luisita noticed that her father appeared extremely tired. She mentioned it to him. "No, of course not. I'm feeling fine," he reassured her.

Around the table at Cavé's, Haas's face suddenly stiffened and his hand groped for the silverware. They called the Jockey Club's carriage in which he had arrived. Two weeks later he had another attack. This was followed, a few months later, by a powerful and final third attack, which finished him off in a matter of hours. It was July 14—Bastille Day.

ONE MORNING I RECEIVED two letters concerning the death of Charles Haas. The first was from the government records office:

Certificate of Death

Established on July 15, in the year nineteen hundred and two, at ten o'clock in the morning. Charles Haas, sixty-nine years of age, honorary inspector of fine arts, born in Paris, died in his home, at 85 avenue de Villiers, yesterday, at nine-thirty in the morning. His father and mother are deceased and their names are unknown. Bachelor. Prepared by us . . . upon the statement provided by Noël Perret, twenty-eight years old, profession unknown, 19 rue du Colisée, son-in-law, and Antony de Beuker . . . , friend.

The second, a small, handwritten note, came from the parish of Saint-François-de-Sales in Paris:

On this day of July 16, in the year nineteen hundred and two, the body of Charles Haas, deceased on July 14, seventy years of age, residing at 85 avenue de Villiers, was presented to the church. No. 120, 2nd class, administered.

From Monsieur and Madame Émile Straus, Trouville, to Madame Noël Perret Haas:

> We are deeply moved, Madame, by the death of your poor father, of whom we were so fond, and I want you to know that we share in your suffering. Please accept my sympathy in this moment of sorrow.
>
> Geneviève Halévy Straus, 104 rue de Miromesnil

From Alphonse de Rothschild:

> My dear young friend, I share the suffering you now experience with all my heart and know what you are going through in the face of this irreparable loss. Your dear father was so perfect, so tender with you, and the most charming companion. In losing him, I am losing an old and devoted friend, and his memory will be as dear to me as my sense of loss at his death. . . . May God sustain you during this trial, dear young friend, and accept my tender and devoted sympathy.

From an unknown to M. Noël Perret:

> Her unfortunate father was in such a state that his death came as a relief to him. Indeed, those who loved him could only wish to see him delivered from his incurable ills.

IN THE *SEARCH* THERE ARE similar signs of commiseration shown for Swann upon his death. Odette, for example, long after his death, spoke of her memories to the narrator: "Poor Charles, he was so intelligent, so seductive, exactly the kind of man I was fond of." The Guermantes, now more kindly disposed toward

Gilberte, have agreed, in their infinite generosity, to speak to her of her "poor father." Charlus no longer speaks of him other than as "poor Swann." Swann himself confided in his daughter (unaware of the fact that he is mistaken), "I'm so pleased, dear, to have a daughter like you. One day, when I'm no longer around, if they still talk of your poor papa, it will only be with you and because of you."

(In the *Search*, Proust writes "that poor Swann," the way others, in real life, referred to Haas as "that poor Haas." Proust always referred to Haas as "that poor Haas.")

And it was necessary that Swann should deceive himself, delude himself, and that the truth be the very opposite of what he believed. "The woman who should have renewed, if not perpetuated, his memory, hastened to conclude the work of death and forgetfulness." For this deliberate intensification of the "work of death and forgetfulness" conducted by Mademoiselle Gilberte S. Forcheville, Marquise de Saint-Loup, who would become the Duchesse de Guermantes upon Oriane's death, no convincing psychological motivation is provided by Proust. No motivation whatsoever. That's because the reason is extraliterary, outside the field of view. In one sense it is Proust the writer who must hasten "the work of death and forgetfulness," and it is Proust the writer who must appear, the deus ex machina of life and death, the god of oblivion and resurrection, as the irreplaceable engine capable of saving Swann/Haas from oblivion, from the limbo that his brilliant urbanity could do nothing to avert.

I have always wondered why Proust didn't attend Haas's funeral ceremony, which was held on July 15, 1902, in Saint-François-de-Sales in Paris. Was he traveling at the time? Was it because he hadn't been informed? Even though Proust and Haas had a number of acquaintances in common?

There is another mystery, this one quite bizarre. Haas wasn't buried in Père-Lachaise until October 29. So where was he between mid-July and the end of October 1902?

I went to Père-Lachaise to look for his tomb. It was the end of August, but it felt like a bleak autumn day, gray and rainy (a fine, steady English rain). Still, it was mild and I wasn't feeling morose. I stopped at the information desk to get the exact location of the grave: division 28, row 11, alley 37, row 3 of division 29. . . . I was soon in front of a sober chapel, austere, abandoned. I was preoccupied by a cross, on top. And an inscription: Perret-Haas family. I concluded, wrongly, that this couldn't be the tomb of Charles Haas. But after several acrobatic and perilous perambulations around the cenotaphs and thickets, under the steady drizzle, surrounded by a few young tourists with their guidebooks in hand, men alone perhaps looking for women or other men, or maybe nothing, I had to accept the evidence that this was indeed Haas's tomb. The small chapel was obviously sealed. Through the opening in the door, on the right-hand wall, I was able to make out an inscription, a single inscription: Charles Haas, died July 14, 1902, 69 years of age. That was all. I took a photograph of the chapel. Then another at a different angle. As I made my way back to the information desk, I ran across the Javal-Lan family plot. At the time I was unaware that the names were Jewish. I read one of the steles: Adèle Lan, wife of David Singer, deceased September 15, 1827. She was Charles's maternal aunt, the sister of Sophie Lan, his mother. This David Singer, who died on January 19, 1846, had been one of the witnesses at the marriage of Charles's parents, Sophie and Antoine. Another of Sophie's sisters, Julie, born in 1799, deceased on October 2, 1854, had married Léopold Javal, who was born in 1800 and died on May 11, 1873. I later learned that Léopold Javal had been a deputy, a chevalier of the Legion of Honor, an honorary member of the Jewish Aid Society known as the Promised Land, founded in 1854. . . .

(I compiled endless genealogies. It was a bit like a spy game, a *Kriegspiel*, waged against an enemy network, where some rare piece of true information is safely transmitted within a tissue of lies.)

I returned to the information desk, where the employees—

pleasant enough, but jealous of information they felt was confidential, and which they revealed reluctantly—informed me that the Haas plot had been purchased in 1838, the date of Antoine's death. But what I found really astonishing was that in 1902, upon Charles Haas's death, Antoine's body was exhumed. Why? Something told me that a man who had lived, and died, a Jew could not remain in this chapel. So where did Antoine's remains now lie? It wasn't until somewhat later that I would learn what had happened.

Léon Lan. He was born in Réguisheim, along the upper Rhine, in 1768. His father was Lippmann Lan, his mother Esther Poraque. The *Lang* family was listed in the "General classification of Jews tolerated in the province of Alsace," dated July 10, 1784. (Even the name of this administrative document spoke volumes about the status of Jews in ancien régime France: they were *tolerated*. Later, at the time of the Vichy government, another status would be applied.)

Léon Lan married Jeannette Cerf Bodenheim in Paris, on 22 Vendémiaire Year II (October 13, 1793). The couple settled at 11 rue de la Victoire, but soon moved to 6 rue Saint-Merry.

Léon Lan died in Rouen on January 8, 1823. He was fifty-five. On January 13, 1823, Madame Léon Lan, his widow, acquired from the city of Paris a plot including four meters of land in the Cimetière de l'Est. On the deed, which is dated November 9, 1844, we read, "The word Israelite is written in red ink in the comments column." Most likely the document was altered at some later date. The plot bore the number 80378.

Sophie, the daughter of Léon Lan and Jeannette C. Bodenheim, was born on 11 Primaire Year X (December 22, 1801). She married Antoine Haas on March 22, 1824. The couple moved to 21 rue Laffitte. Antoine died on December 9, 1838.

On December 11, Sophie Lan, widow of Antoine Haas, acquired a two-meter plot in the Cimetière de l'Est "to establish the particular and perpetual resting place" of her deceased husband. Plot number 60441.

Sophie's mother, Jeannette, died on November 7, 1844. She was buried in plot 80378, which she had purchased in 1823, where her husband, Léon Lan, was buried.

Sophie Lan died on December 10, 1870. It was her son, our Charles, I assume (he wondered if he would be admitted to the Jockey Club; he had just ended his affair with Sarah), who accompanied her to her final resting place, where she joined her mother and father, but not Antoine, who was resting peacefully in the adjoining plot.

On February 8, 1902, Jesusa Maria Josefa Luisa Ramirez de Arellano Haas, then living with her father, Charles Nathan Haas, at 85 avenue de Villiers, wed Noël Perret, residing at 19 rue du Colisée, Paris. Witnesses for the marriage, on the bride's side, which is the only side we're interested in here, included Victor Masséna, Prince d'Essling, Duc de Rivoli, sixty-six years old, property owner, chevalier of the Legion of Honor, 8 rue Jean-Goujon, and Alfred, Marquis du Lair d'Allemand, sixty-eight years old, property owner, chevalier of the Legion of Honor, 99 rue des Petits-Champs.

(In spite of everything, I still had doubts about this Alfred's identity. Swann/Haas's closest friend was the Marquis du Lau d'Allemans. I hoped it was simply a poor transcription.)

Luisa and Noël moved in to 15 avenue Matignon. Among the couple's wedding gifts were 240 de Beers gold mine shares deposited with Crédit Lyonnais. I didn't try to find out what this would represent in modern currency or even to compare it with the amount the narrator refers to when discussing Gilberte's dowry, which, in the *Search*, is sometimes eighty million francs, sometimes a hundred million.

Charles dies on July 14, 1902.

On the twenty-sixth day of that same month, Luisa, in family plot 80378 of the Jewish cemetery (acquired by her paternal great-grandmother in 1823), had the following work performed: "Dismantle and remove any burial material for the exhumation of 1. Léon Lan, 2. Jeannette C. Bodenheim, 3. Sophie Lan." On the same day, she had the following work done for the other plot (60441, acquired by her grandmother in 1838): "Dismantle and remove any burial material for the exhumation of Monsieur Antoine Haas."

On August 25, for this same plot, she had the following work performed: "Excavation and construction of a crypt with six compartments for coffins plus the required clear space." On October 9, as the beneficiary of her paternal great-grandparents, she asked to exchange the four-meter plot (80378) and the two-meter plot (60441) against a contiguous four-and-a-half-meter plot.

October 24: construction of the chapel.

October 29: burial of the body of Charles Haas, arriving from the Church of Saint-François-de-Sales.

I now realized why Charles's corpse remained for so long— from July 15 to October 29—at the Church of Saint-François-de-Sales before being buried in Père-Lachaise. Luisa wanted her father to have a distinguished tomb. A Christian tomb. A chapel. Emptied, one would imagine, of all that Jewish "burial material" for the sake of the man who would, unknown to her, soon become Proust's immortal swan. This material was the source of a twofold, reciprocal embarrassment. Both for the converted and for his Jewish parents. Luisa cleared the way for a new start. I'm not sure if I would call this a new start in life, however, since we are dealing with death. Charles, in the chapel with six compartments for coffins "plus the required clear space," was supposed to rest alone. And he did remain alone, for other members of the family were buried at M—— in the south of France. His is a sad, depressing monument that no visitor before me is likely to have gone to see. And why would they? For the real tomb of Swann/Haas—a cathedral of words—is worth far more.

SWANN IS A CONVERTED JEW. Some (Madame de Gallardon confided as much to her cousin, the Princesse de Laumes) claimed that his parents, and even his grandparents, had already converted. Personally, I am unaware of the circumstances under which Haas became a Catholic. I'm not certain it occurred around 1880, when he met the highly devout Adélaïde at the home of the no less devout Annette de Poilly. Why did she care about his conversion since there was no question of his marrying her? Of course, it's true that he wanted his daughter to be raised as a good Christian. He encouraged her to say her little prayers, to pray for her little papa, to send him her little pictures. It wouldn't hurt her and might even help relieve some of the anguish she felt—or so her father said—from her nervousness, which she inherited from her distant maternal relative, Juana la Loca. Although her "nervousness" could be attributed to more immediate causes: she grew up without knowing who her mother and father were. This alone would have been cause enough for her "nervousness," not to mention Juana, the mad Iberian.

At the home of the Princesse R———, quai d'Anjou, I copied the touching letters from the young Luisita to her father (in spite of—for me, in any case—their inevitable Catholic pieties). I lit a cigarette. I also happened to overhear a bitter, highly animated discussion between the princess and her maid, who was asking for a week's worth of unpaid wages. The princess, her calendar in hand, insisted that she had paid them.

Reading Luisita's childish letters, written from the Convent of the Assumption in Lourdes, or while traveling during the school vacation with her nurse, Miss Rudd (Palais Costanzo, San Benedetto, March 5, 189—; Lugano, July 18, 189—; Genoa, May 6, 189—; Modena, October 12, 189—), or from Folembray, at the home of Madame de Poilly, in the company of Madame Ollivier, I inevitably thought of my own daughter. I told myself that I had little intention of sending her to a convent . . . or telling her that I wasn't her father.

The princess brought me her albums. Worn, faded, stiff photographs that were dead to me and to everyone else. The people who appeared in them had been dead for decades. The princess herself was still able to name a few of those individuals—who were really "somebodies" in their own time—because her grandmother, Luisita, may have pointed them out to her. But it is unlikely that her son was able to do so. And there was no reason for him to worry about it much either.

Then there were the ardent letters from Sarah Bernhardt. There were others, almost illegible, from Victorien Sardou, about a play by Haas, apparently now lost, which Sardou appeared to judge rather severely: "I have never encountered more talent," Sardou wrote to Haas in Arcachon around 1864 or 1865, "used to such poor effect."

An air of frivolity, of insignificance hung over that collection of papers. And if Haas, at bottom, and in spite of Proust . . . I don't dare continue. The whole thing, I admit, exasperated me. Almost to the point of suffering. From time to time, the princess, her right wrist in a cast from a recent fall, entered the room where I had settled, sat near me, picked up a piece of paper at random, tried in vain to decipher it, and put it back on the table with a sigh. Had I found something interesting? Hardly. Oh well, she suspected as much. She had warned me during our first conversation on the phone. Concerning Haas, there was nothing to say. Elegant, seductive, a dandy, a man of the world, a dilettante, an art lover. . . . What was I going to do with so little to go on? I had no idea. She sighed, then stood and excused herself, since she had to leave. She said, "I trust you will put everything back in order when you're done?" I understood the implication of her comment and assured her I was no collector.

Coda

To CLAIM THAT *IN SEARCH OF LOST TIME* ORIGINATES WITH SWANN would be both true and impossible. It's impossible because the *Search* is a real object and can't be confused with "the book not yet written," the one planned by the narrator. Just as Marcel, quite obviously, is not Proust. However, the statement is indeed true. The narrator says so explicitly: "The substance of my experience, which will be the substance of my book, I took from Swann." He lists his sources: Gilberte, Balbec (where Swann encourages him to go), Albertine, the Guermantes, et cetera, "so that it was through Swann that I was now at the home of the Prince de Guermantes, where the idea for my book suddenly came to me (which meant that I was indebted to Swann not only for the material but for the decision)."

Indeed, Proust-Marcel is fascinated by Swann/Haas. Yet this fascination does not exclude lucidity. For the narrator's desire to write also arose *to spite* Swann. And if there is one character in the book who irritates him, it's Swann. Because our greatest irritation arises from those who attract us. Otherwise, we are merely amused, or indifferent. For the person who irritates us casts us into shadow, seduces us, and exasperates us by their seduction. Consequently, as if to protect ourselves, we seek out—at any cost and with all our strength—the faults, flaws, and weaknesses of our all-powerful seducer. And we find them. We find them because we are looking for them. We tell ourselves that such perfection in life is simply not possible. It exists only in works of art. And a "life" is not a work of art. This small truth took the narrator a long time to discover—the time it would take Proust to write the *Search*. He found it through Swann but also in spite of him.

Swann irritates the narrator so often because he has wounded him. When he is in love with Gilberte, he worries because Swann doesn't speak to him. After making inquiries, the narrator discovers that the young woman's parents are not "fond" of him, they feel he'll be a bad influence on their daughter. The narrator then picks up his pen and writes a letter to Swann, confiding in him everything he feels about him, to correct his "absurd error." It's nothing more than a simple misunderstanding, something Marcel will be able to clear up. There's nothing complicated about it; the facts will speak for themselves. The reason that Swann doesn't speak to his daughter's young friend when he comes to get her in the Champs-Élysées is far simpler, far more banal, and has nothing to do with any misunderstanding and is not as easily clarified: Swann is simply indifferent about Marcel, just as Haas most likely was about Proust. He says it himself, many pages later, while recollecting Swann/Haas, "And yet, dear Charles Swann, although I never knew you very well when I was so young and you were so close to death . . . the youngster you must have considered a little idiot." No, it wasn't a question of any "bad influence" but of a "little idiot." It's a different kind of pain when a man as prestigious as Swann considers you to be nothing but a piece of crap. But this prestige of his, was it really all that justified? If I were in Marcel's place, I think that's what I would try to find out. And that's exactly what he does. And no, you have to admit that there aren't that many reasons for him, Swann, to be venerated, or sanctified, or idolized. Why is he so interested in certain people in the first place, such as, "a certain great lady, now déclassé"? Simply because she had once been Liszt's mistress or because a Balzac novel had been dedicated to her? If he bought a drawing, it was because Chateaubriand had described it. He was also contaminated by the Guermantes's mentality. He placed "wit" above intelligence. To him, Brichot is a pedant (in spite of his considerable knowledge) and Elstir a boor (in spite of his genius). Then there was his absurd snobbism. What if he was the friend of the Comte de Paris or the Prince of Wales! It meant nothing. The princes, the true princes, are not snobs. They believe they are "so far above anyone who does not share their ancestry that great lords and the bourgeoisie appear to them, since they are so far beneath them, to be on the same level." And then there is the glaring contradiction between what he says and what he does, claiming that the balls given by the Princesse de Léon were unimportant even though he spent his life pursuing such pleasures. He was limited in his judgments and tastes as well, repeating, like everyone else, that Bergotte was a delightful wit, but ultimately incapable of saying why he mattered—namely, because he was a great writer. In reality, did Swann ever show himself to be a superior mind?

The narrator continuously tries to reestablish the hierarchy of values, the discrimination of attitudes. Swann's position is certainly ambivalent—sometimes he sides with Marcel, concerning his character, and sometimes with Haas, concerning his worldliness. But it's clear that the narrator is someplace else: he sides entirely with Vinteuil and creativity. A creative Swann/Haas would be impossible. He would be a "monster" unlike anything nature has ever produced. Swann's limited research on Vermeer will culminate in nothing. Haas's play exists only as a draft, a project. But what does it matter? What made Swann/Haas happy was the ability to please. And to frequent his Cercle. His circles. He was at the center of a number of circles. The circles of a circular life. Which he loved. Which loved him. He was not saving himself for a different life. He had only one life, and how sad it would have been to leave it prematurely.

As for myself, like those sentimental films whose final image displays a hand closing the volume it had opened at the beginning, or a cluster of people gathered around the grave of a loved one whose destiny has just been described and who have now accompanied the body to its final resting place, I saw my own book close above a grave. It was probably time that I started thinking about myself, about what I would do with my life, which has been, until now, no more than "an empty frame waiting for a masterpiece." I had to get to work, abandon Haas to the eternal solitude of the cemetery of Père-Lachaise, surrounded by so many who are unaware that his grave merits a parting glance. I had to abandon Swann as well, who has been visited, pampered, solicited, and loved by readers for so long. I was also unable to ignore the ingratitude, the inherent injustice of the twinned destinies of Swann and Haas, initially so parallel, then so divergent. No, Proust did not save Haas, as I had first believed. And he tells us why: "A book is an enormous cemetery, where most of the names have been worn from the gravestones." For some obscure reason, I had tried to reinscribe the name, to rename Charles Haas. I was unable to accept the fact that his name would die, as any other name for that matter. I had wanted to bring him back from anonymity. For it was really this sense of anonymity that I refused to accept. My own future anonymity. If Haas, so celebrated, so courted, so famous, could fall into such terrifying oblivion, what about me, what about my name? Would my daughter behave like Gilberte? Was there any way to stop her? I had to write a book so that my name would endure, so that it was not attached only to this contingent being one might pass on the street or call on the phone, but to an object that was clearly outside him, one that could be seen and touched without knowing who I was, something separate, and that would perhaps ensure, when I am no longer around, that I continue to live.